HKAC

MAY 2011

HOSTAS
An essential guide

HOSTAS
An essential guide

Richard Ford

THE CROWOOD PRESS

First published in 2010 by
The Crowood Press Ltd
Ramsbury, Marlborough
Wiltshire SN8 2HR

www.crowood.com

British Library Cataloguing-in-Publication Data
A catalogue record for this book is available from the British Library.

ISBN 978 1 84797 218 7

Frontispiece: Hosta Demonstration Borders at Park Green Nurseries in Suffolk.

Typeset by Servis Filmsetting Ltd, Stockport, Cheshire
Printed and bound in India by Replika Press Pvt Ltd

Contents

ACKNOWLEDGEMENT

Without my wife Mary,
I would never have started our Hosta Nursery
and without her participation
over the last 25 years
I would never have been able to write this book.

Preface

My wife and I first grew Hostas in the late 1960s in a totally unsuitable soil. This was a very light sandy loam with pure sand less than 1ft (30cm) down. The varieties were *Hosta* 'Thomas Hogg' (now *Hosta undulata* variety *albomarginata*) and *Hosta fortunei* variety *albopicta* which are both still widely available. Against the odds they did very well and these first efforts encouraged me to try more of the available varieties.

Over the years our borders filled up with Hostas and many other herbaceous perennials, inevitably leading to a surplus of plants. We could not bring ourselves to throw them away and we started to pot up and sell the plants we no longer needed.

The decision to start our own nursery followed quite naturally and late in 1982 we moved to suitable premises taking with us our collection of Hostas which by then had grown to forty-five varieties. Since then we have very much extended our Hosta collection, made Hostas our livelihood, exhibited them very successfully at major shows and raised and registered our own varieties.

If nothing else we have learnt over the years how to grow Hostas in our garden and in containers and how to get on top of their only serious predators, the dreaded slugs and snails. My aim now is to pass on as much as possible of this practical information in this book to help you achieve good results with Hostas in your garden.

On finishing with school and National Service I studied Botany at University as I always wanted employment, which would allow me to work mainly out of doors. I remember only too well our first lecture – the Professor surprised us all by saying, 'Whatever you have learnt so far, forget it. Now we will start again!' I often feel that this very much applies to Hostas, as after speaking to many thousands of gardeners over the years, I believe them to be a misunderstood genus. Most of us have strong preconceived ideas about how and where Hostas should be grown. Historically, they have been relegated to the damp and shady parts of the garden. Hostas deserve better than this as they are able to thrive in other places as well. I hope that the advice and information in this book will perhaps encourage and enable some of you to rethink and grow super Hostas in more varied situations.

NOMENCLATURE OF HOSTAS

The United Kingdom's Advisory Committee on Nomenclature and Taxonomy comprises experts who advise on the naming of plants in cultivation. The Royal Horticultural Society holds a regularly updated horticultural database which is used for their annual publication *The RHS Plant Finder*, and the Hosta names used in this publication have been used throughout this book.

It is accepted that some differences will be found by overseas readers. A simple example is the use of *Hosta tokudama* in the UK, whereas other authorities would use *Hosta* 'Tokudama', since they would regard it as a variety rather than a species.

CHAPTER 1

From the wild to our gardens

ORIGINS OF HOSTAS

Hostas, in common with many other plants grown in British gardens, originated mainly in Japan, but were also found in China and Korea. While Hostas had been grown in Japanese gardens for hundreds of years, they did not arrive in Britain until nearly 1800. This was a comparatively late introduction as, by this time, a very wide range of plants were already being grown in our gardens.

It is generally accepted that there are around fifty species of Hosta in the wild – the uncertainty is because some so-called species may be or have been proved to be naturally occurring varieties. Even for a trained botanist it is difficult to see how this can be solved with any certainty. What is important is that these species are not all found in the same locations or in the same growing situations. They are found in the open, in the shade, and in partially-shaded areas bordering woodlands. They also grow in high, mountainous areas in thin gritty soils in rock crevices and even clinging to sheer rock faces. They are also found in fertile soils in woodland, valleys, and in marshy places. With this very wide range of habitats, it has to be accepted that the preferred planting positions of varieties derived from these wild plants are not necessarily going to be the same for all Hosta varieties available to gardeners. The more time one spends with Hostas, the less one can generalize about them, and the differences between varieties are not just in appearance but also in their behaviour and performance under varying garden conditions.

Hosta 'Big Daddy', a very popular variety with its blue leaves and white flowers, but not as large as the name suggests.

THE NAMING OF PLANTS

There must be a method of naming plants that is acceptable throughout the world, and the binomial system devised by Carl Linnaeus has provided the answer. This uses Latin names for the Genus (the generic name) and the species (the specific name) such as *Hosta plantaginea*. Latin is used, as it would be impossible to agree on a language that would be an acceptable alternative, but it is not without advantages as when one understands the system, the Latin names are descriptive for both the genus and the species. The name *Hosta* was given for Dr Nicolaus Thomas Host, an Austrian physician and botanist, and *plantaginea* means 'a plantain-like plant'. We also have names for cultivated plants (abbreviated to 'cultivar' and cv.), which in the case of Hostas may be registered with the central authority and like the generic and specific names are then recognized and used throughout the world.

In addition plants also have common English names, and in Britain and elsewhere Hostas have appropriately been named as Plantain Lilies. Different names, often in foreign languages, would be used in other countries and would not always be recognized in Britain. The Latin names are therefore essential for the international recognition of plants, though regrettably, botanists do find valid scientific reasons for changing Latin names from time to time when a plant is found to have been placed in an incorrect genus or species. The same Linnaean system is used for all plant and animal life from the tiniest micro-organisms (for example baker's yeast – *Saccharomyces cerevisiae*) to the greatest dinosaurs (*Tyrannosaurus rex*).

Species may be defined as groups of individual plants which can breed to produce 'similar' offspring having a number of defined characters, and a Genus (plural genera) as a group of species which share easily recognisable features and are genetically related, and which in the wild would normally only breed within the genus. Cultivars (cultivated varieties) are normally the result of breeding between different species within the same genus, and occasionally from different genera.

Nomenclature can differ slightly between nations but all names are still recognisable. The Latin names used throughout this book are as detailed in the Royal Horticultural Society's book *Plant Finder* which is updated annually.

A considerable number of these species are available commercially and some remain popular garden plants. These include the following.

Hosta gracillima

This is one of the smallest species and can form a dense clump of small glossy green leaves with wavy margins and lavender flowers on stems up to 15in (38cm) tall.

Hosta minor

Another small clump-forming species with small medium to green smooth leaves, with purple flowers on long stems up to 20in (50cm) tall.

Hosta nigrescens

This is an elegant, very large and upright species which at our nursery (Park Green Nursery) produces a leaf clump just over 2ft (60cm) tall. The flowers are very pale lavender on extremely tall stems over 3ft (90cm) tall. It is well worth growing in the garden as an eye-catching feature in any border. The upright growth of this species is a particularly useful feature as it does make the plant less accessible to slugs and snails.

Hosta nigrescens, a show specimen growing at our Nursery. Still a popular variety for the garden and spectacular in a container.

Hosta plantaginea, with its pure white flowers in August. This species is the parent of many scented flowered Hosta varieties.

Hosta plantaginea

This is a species which is very much in demand, particularly as a parent for cultivars with scented flowers. It was named in 1789 – in the first instance as *Hemerocallis japonica*, though the species is native to China. It is a very distinctive plant with smooth, light green leaves which are glossy and heart-shaped; the flowers are very large, pure white and strongly scented. In America the flowers are reported to reach a length of 6in (15cm) but it is unlikely that they would grow as large as this in Britain. They flower late from mid August almost into October. The best available form of the species is *Hosta plantaginea* variety *japonica* (previously *grandiflora*), and many cultivated varieties are derived from this species.

It is arguable as to whether *Hosta plantaginea* variety *japonica* should be described as a separate variety, and recognized American authorities suggest that it is identical to *Hosta plantaginea*.

Hosta sieboldiana

This species is often called *sieboldii* by gardeners but the two are distinct and very different. Both are named for the celebrated plant collector Phillip von Siebold (1796–1866) who did much throughout his life to make Hostas such popular garden plants. *Hosta sieboldiana* produces a large clump over 2ft (60cm) tall and well over 4ft (120cm) wide with large, thick bluish-green leaves which are slightly corrugated. The flowers are near white with a tinge of purple in mid season. The best-known cultivar is *Hosta sieboldiana* variety *elegans* which is very widely available, and which has paler flowers and bluer, more heavily-corrugated foliage. This variety is the parent of many modern Hosta cultivars.

Hosta sieboldii

This has been maintained as a species but it is likely that it originated from a green leaved Hosta. It is a small to medium variety, previously known under several other names, and to list these would only cause confusion. *Hosta sieboldii* forms a small dense clump of foliage about 12in (30cm) tall comprising lance-shaped leaves which are mid-green with a narrow white margin. The flowers are mid-purple standing about 15in (38cm) tall. There are many cultivars arising from this species.

Hosta ventricosa growing in the Botanical Gardens in Dublin.

Hosta ventricosa

This, like *Hosta plantaginea,* is also a native of China, and is a large Hosta with the foliage mound about 2ft (60cm) tall and over 4ft (120cm) wide. It has heart-shaped, rather glossy leaves, and very attractive dark purple flowers on tall stalks.

There are many significant varieties from *Hosta ventricosa* including the two oldest, which are worth including, particularly as they have retained the spectacular flowers of their parent:

Hosta ventricosa variety aureamaculata

In spring this has gold-centred leaves, which darken to fully green by the end of the year. The young plants can be difficult to grow but once a plant is established it produces a superb clump every year.

Hosta 'Aureomarginata' (ventricosa)

This has the dark green leaves of its parent, but with broad yellow margins which lighten to creamy white during the summer. Before the advent of more popular, gold-edged types, this was a very popular variety.

Hosta venusta

A small species producing a dense mound of mid-green leaves. The flowers are purple and, like many of the small Hostas, are produced on tall flower stalks. This variety is described more fully in Chapter 8.

A number of other early Hostas previously given specific names are now regarded as cultivars. Again some of these are available commercially, but their importance is due to them being the precursors of many of our present and future cultivars. Of particular interest amongst these varieties from the wild are as follows.

Hosta fortunei

This was named for the Scottish plant hunter Robert Fortune who was active in the mid-1800s. The variety produces a large mound of quite large, medium-green leaves and pale lavender flowers about 30in (75cm) tall. Not very interesting, but again its importance is in the many varieties raised from it as well as the original *fortunei*-type varieties such as:

Hosta fortunei variety albomarginata

This is larger than its parent and with white-margined, mid-green leaves.

Hosta fortunei variety albopicta and Hosta fortunei variety aureomarginata

These two are important currently available varieties and will be described in Chapter 8.

Hosta fortunei variety albopicta form aurea

This is again similar to the parent but less vigorous and with leaves that emerge bright gold in the spring and fade to green within a few weeks.

Hosta fortunei variety hyacinthina

This is also similar to the parent but with slightly bluer leaves. It also has a pencil line of white around the leaf margin. From this variety over twenty variegated forms have been raised, including our own introduction, *Hosta* 'Ron Damant'.

Hosta lancifolia

This is another native of China and one of the earliest to be introduced into Europe. It is a fast growing, medium-sized variety with lance shaped, quite dark green leaves, and it produces many purple flowers up to 18in (45cm) tall over a long time-period in late summer. It has been suggested that it is, or has been, the most commonly planted Hosta, but has been superseded by many more modern varieties.

Hosta tokudama

This Hosta is another variety from Japan introduced to Britain in the mid-1800s. It is a medium-sized plant with thick, rounded and corrugated blue-green leaves. The flowers are nearly white and reach up to 2ft (60cm) tall. From this one Hosta have come two important early varieties *Hostas tokudama* form *aureonebulosa* and *tokudama* form *flavocircinalis*. They will be described in Chapter 8 as they also are popular and readily available varieties, which in turn are the parents of other important varieties.

Hosta undulata

This variety is from Japan and was originally known as the striped Hosta. It was one of the first recognized variegated Hostas, and was imported into Europe in 1829. It was for many years regarded as the best centre-variegated Hosta available. In Britain this centre-variegated variety has been separated into *Hosta undulata* variety *undulata* (previously *Hosta undulata mediovariegata*) and *Hosta undulata* variety *univittata*, which is slightly more vigorous and has a narrower splash of white in the leaf centre.

Another very important variety is *undulata* variety *albomarginata* which, as the Latin name defines, has green leaves with white margins. In its day it was quite a breakthrough and was brought from Japan to the United States in 1875 and was cultivated there and in Europe as *Funkia*, later *Hosta* 'Thomas Hogg'. It is still sold widely but is becoming less popular due to the introduction of many vastly superior, white margined Hostas.

The first of these Hostas to arrive in Britain were *Hosta plantaginea* and *Hosta ventricosa,* just before 1800. Both of these, particularly the former, are parents of modern varieties. At that time the generic name Hosta had not been proposed and these two varieties were first given the generic name *Hemerocallis,* the Day Lily Genus, and included with them in the Lily Family (*Liliaceae*). Hostas were also known briefly under other generic names including *Funkia, Niobe* and *Aletris*, and these names are used in some old gardening and scientific literature.

Fortunately agreement was reached for the use of the generic name Hosta and it is now the only name used. Hostas were soon considered to be of sufficient importance to form their own family, the *Hostaceae*.

EARLY HYBRIDIZING OF HOSTAS

European plant collectors were able to gain access to China and Japan from the early 1820s and they sent Hostas to Europe in much greater quantities and in a wider range of species and varieties. These Hostas were both from the wild and also varieties already in cultivation in their countries of origin. By the mid-1800s Hostas were being grown in gardens in the USA and American plant collectors visited Japan to again increase the availability of Hostas.

Important milestones in 1968 were both the foundation of the American Hosta Society and also the appointment of the University of Minnesota in the USA as the International Registration Authority for the genus Hosta. Responsibility for the Registration of Hostas now rests with the American Hosta Society.

Hosta undulata variety *undulata*, one of the earliest available centre variegated Hostas.

THE AMERICAN HOSTA SOCIETY

This Society has an excellent website (*see* Further Information) which gives a great deal of useful information on Hostas. It needs to be borne in mind that Hostas do generally grow larger in the United States; colours of the flowers can be slightly different; and some of their pests and diseases are (fortunately for us) not of significant importance in Britain. At present, there is a huge amount of movement of Hostas between countries and between continents which does inevitably lead to the spread of pests and diseases, which are endemic to the country of origin.

Another useful web address is the Hosta Library (*see* Further Information); this is again operated from the United States, and contains much very useful information and a range of photographs of many Hosta varieties. Some are of juvenile plants and occasionally there is variation between individual pictures of the same variety, but the value of the website far outweighs these shortcomings.

The growth of registered Hostas has been quite rapid, with just three in 1969, then reaching fifty-two new Hosta varieties registered in 1978, and rising to a maximum of nearly 400 in 1999, falling to 150 in 2008 though rising again later. Sadly, fewer than sixty per cent of Hosta cultivars have been registered. The process of registration requires the completion of an uncomplicated form describing the diagnostic features of the new variety, supplying photographs and paying a very small fee. Full details are available from the American Hosta Society website (*see* Further Information). Important early introductions to Britain from the USA include *Hostas* 'Frances Williams', 'Honeybells', 'Krossa Regal', 'Royal Standard', and 'Thomas Hogg' which are still very popular more than thirty years later.

We are fortunate that important pioneering work on hybridizing Hostas has been carried out in Britain. The most notable has been by Eric Smith who, by crossing *Hosta sieboldiana* variety *elegans* (a large blue-green leaved plant) with *Hosta tardiflora* (a medium sized, late flowering, dark green leaved plant) produced the 'tardianas', a range of superb blue and green leaved varieties. These vary in plant size and leaf shape and include

Hosta 'Royal Standard' catching the sun to light up a shaded position at Green Island Gardens, Ardleigh, Essex.

Hosta 'Krossa Regal', an elegant upright variety, growing in a Chelsea Show garden.

Hosta 'Halcyon', probably the most popular medium sized blue leaved Hosta.

the ever-popular *Hosta* 'Halcyon'. It is debatable whether this is the bluest of the 'tardianas' and possibly 'Hadspen Blue' or others can claim the title. There are many other 'tardianas' varying in size and leaf shape and colour. Popular varieties include the following:

- 'Blue Ice' – a very small variety.
- 'Blue Moon', 'Blue Skies', and Dorset Blue' – small to medium varieties.
- 'Hadspen Heron' – medium with narrow leaves.
- 'Blue Wedgwood' – medium with spade-shaped leaves.

Eric Smith died in 1986 and one of his unnamed Hostas was registered a year later as *Hosta* 'Eric Smith' in his memory. Although this is probably one of the least blue of the 'Tardiana' series, it is however a very handsome plant making a uniform, medium-sized clump, which generally lasts well into the autumn.

The 'tardianas' and particularly *Hosta* 'Halcyon' have through their seedlings and other offspring produced some of the most outstanding Hosta varieties of modern times and this in itself is a tribute to Eric Smith's pioneering work.

Eric Smith was also involved with the introduction of other important and still popular varieties including *Hosta* 'Gold Haze', a large, golden leaved variety and *Hosta* 'Snowden', a very large spectacular variety with sage green leaves and pure white flowers. These are both important varieties and are fully described in Chapter 8.

FURTHER DEVELOPMENT OF HOSTAS

Apart from the efforts of Eric Smith only a modest proportion of Hosta varieties have been raised outside the USA. Other countries where hybridizers have been active include Britain, Holland, Germany, Belgium, New Zealand, and Japan, the country of origin. The vast majority of modern Hosta varieties have been raised by American growers and we are indebted to them for the large number of outstanding varieties which they have introduced. Many of these spectacular varieties have crossed the Atlantic to Britain and increasingly to other countries in both the Northern and Southern Hemispheres.

Hostas have always been regarded as damp- and

shade-loving plants, whereas they are better described as damp and shade tolerant yet suitable for growing in more open and sunny positions. The reason is historical; when Hostas first arrived in Britain, some were grown as 'stove' or conservatory plants, but the gardeners in the 1800s soon found that Hostas were hardy and grew well in their gardens and were particularly useful for growing in continuous shade and in damp soils. From that time until recently most of the books, magazines, and media presenters have promoted them predominantly for this sole purpose.

If one suggested that 1,000 people were asked to define Hostas in a single sentence, 999 are likely to reply: 'A plant which grows in damp shady places, and whose leaves are shredded by slugs and snails!' Fortunately many people now realize how this has limited the usefulness and popularity of Hostas. It is not proving easy to convince gardeners that Hostas can be grown anywhere except in the shade. However, there is now increasing evidence that Hostas are being used more and more in open and sunny positions. Because Hostas can be divided so easily, gardeners have experimented with their surplus divisions, and have been agreeably surprised to find they can perform well in more sunny and open positions where they would not previously have been expected to grow. To again quote one of my University lecturers – 'We may think we know all the answers, but the plant is always right.' How true!

The gardening public who visit garden shows, botanical gardens, stately homes and open gardens will have become used to seeing Hostas, not only in the expected shaded positions but also in more open and sunny situations. Very few of these gardens fail to include Hostas in their plantings nowadays. It has frequently been suggested that Hostas are fashionable but we have found that they have steadily increased in popularity over the years. The one event that significantly increased this interest is when people made a serious move towards growing Hostas in pots and other containers.

A survey carried out in the year 2000 showed Hostas to be the tenth most popular perennial in British gardens. Since the top nine were perennials grown primarily for their flowers, we may fairly say that Hostas are the top foliage perennial in Britain. In America however, they have become the most popular perennial and as a result they are propagated and grown on a massive scale throughout the USA and Europe to meet the demand.

Many Royal Horticultural Society Awards of Garden Merit have been granted to Hostas, which

Several Hosta varieties growing in a Chelsea Show garden.

in trials proved to be exceptionally garden-worthy plants. Unfortunately it has been nearly twenty years since Hostas have been evaluated and many of our modern varieties are just as good, and frequently better, than those with the award. Just one variety, the outstanding *Hosta* 'June', has been granted the award in 2004. As a result this prestigious award can be very misleading.

To promote British interest in the two genera the British Hosta and Hemerocallis Society (BHHS) was founded in 1981. The Society celebrated its Silver Jubilee in 2006 and produces an annual Bulletin together with frequent newsletters; arranges garden visits and lectures; encourages and funds research on Hostas and Hemerocallis; and has active Regional Groups. Further information and details of membership are given in the Society's website (*see* Further Information). In Britain, the Plant Heritage (National Council for the Conservation of Plants and Gardens) encourages nurseries, private gardeners and other organizations to hold national collections of plant genera. Several such collections for Hostas are held in the United Kingdom, and are also listed on the BHHS website.

In the USA, the Minnesota Arboretum holds a large collection of Hostas. Quite a number of American nurserymen also hold very large collections and such is their popularity that there are many gardens with significant collections and now over sixty regional and local Hosta Societies and groups exist. The Dutch Hosta Society was founded in 1989 and there is a very fine Hosta Collection at the Trompenberg Arboretum on the outskirts of Rotterdam.

AVAILABILITY OF HOSTAS IN BRITAIN

Despite their popularity in British gardens, it is not always possible to easily locate sources of good Hosta plants to buy. The larger garden centres and nurseries seldom stock many Hostas, and when they do these are very often the older varieties. While these will still make good garden plants, it is the newer varieties which are the more attractive and garden-worthy plants and which are more difficult to obtain.

The best source for these plants is a Hosta specialist plant nursery, of which only a few exist in Britain and the rest of Europe. Fortunately these days, through modern technology and the increase in the number of good flower and garden shows

Part of the Hosta Collection at the Trompenberg Arboretum near Rotterdam in Holland.

and plant sales, attended by specialist growers, the situation is much improved.

Suitable sources of information on how and where to obtain Hostas are as follows:

- The British Hosta and Hemerocallis Society website lists member nurseries who can supply a range of modern Hosta varieties, as well as varieties of Hemerocallis. The website also gives links to the Hosta National Collection holders, and officers of the Society.
- The Royal Horticultural Society publishes every year an invaluable book entitled *RHS Plant Finder*. This lists several tens of thousands of plants and over 600 places where they can be purchased. It includes over 1,600 varieties of Hosta. The disadvantages are that sometimes only one or two nurseries (often situated at the other side of the country) may be listed as being able to supply a particular variety; also, because the number of available plants for a new variety may be very limited, none may be immediately available at the time of asking. It is, despite this, a very useful publication and most major specialist nurseries make a point of ensuring that their varieties are included.
- An online facility to search for specific varieties is also offered under the Royal Horticultural Society which can be accessed through their website (see list at back of book) and the home page will direct you to the *RHS Plant Finder* and the Search facility. *RHS Nursery Finder* can also be used to search for a particular nursery by name or by location.
- A general Internet search can also be used for a Hosta variety by name or Hosta nurseries in general. It is only too easy to place an online order for Hosta plants to be mailed to you at more or less any time of year. Ordering plants by post is not always a popular option as people have been disappointed by the size and quality of the plants they receive. We have to fall back on the old adage that 'you get what you pay for' and regrettably plants offered at a very low cost may turn out to be the wrong variety and/or very small. The genuine specialists should quote a fair price for a plant that is of a size suitable for planting straight into the garden. It is not a good idea to buy small

'plugs' because their chances of survival are not always particularly good as often they have an inadequately developed root system. It is also wise to purchase plants from a nursery based in the country where you live as delays in the post are not beneficial to the well-being of the plant. Having said that, Hostas do travel very well in the post particularly during dormancy. Our nursery regularly sends live plants by post for ten months of the year to many countries of the world. It is very seldom that these plants fail to grow well when planted in their new gardens, but careful packaging is essential.

- Best of all is to visit one of the major flower and garden shows, when there are generally up to three or even more specialist Hosta growers, staging exhibits of mature plants and selling young plants which can be taken home then and there.
- Specialist growers will also advertise in the gardening magazines and are very often included in specialist directories listing suppliers of garden plants and sundries.

Care needs to be taken when selecting Hosta plants to purchase. Where there is a choice between several plants in the same size container it is always tempting to choose the plant with the most shoots. Often, where there are more shoots to the pot, they tend to be smaller and sometimes it is preferable to go for plants with few but stronger shoots. You should not be tempted to immediately divide plants with several shoots except when they are older, more well-established plants. What is most important is to choose a plant with a strong, well-developed root system. It is not a bad thing if a Hosta plant has a few roots showing at the base of the pot as Hostas do grow best in a modest size pot, and roots will normally show at the base when a good root system has developed. With most garden plants it is not a good thing to buy any which are 'pot bound', and although Hostas are not unduly worried by this, it is best to avoid Hostas with an excessive amount of root showing at the base of the pot. If roots are showing, or if you can inspect them, ensure that they are firm and white. Browning or blackening of the roots is indicative of fungal rotting.

Choose a healthy turgid plant with firm well

A Park Green Nurseries' stand at the Gardening Scotland Show. The display is on the right, and the selling area on the left.

coloured undamaged foliage and avoid any that have holes in the leaves as this will indicate that they may have been grazed by slugs or snails which may be hiding in, or have laid eggs in the compost. Avoid any that have mottled or distorted foliage as this may indicate the possible presence of a virus. This is not usual but you should be happy with the overall appearance of the plant you intend to buy. Young potted Hostas at point of sale need to be re-potted annually and therefore the presence of established weed in the pot is not a good indication of plant health. Although the price of very young plants might be tempting it is always better to pay more for an older, better established plant. Very young plants may have an inadequate or poorly developed root system, particularly if they are recently weaned, or inadequately weaned micro propagated plants, and these are not suitable for planting straight into the garden.

There can be an element of risk in the purchase of very new varieties. Specialist nurseries are very good at selecting the best of new varieties and growing them on to assess their suitability for British gardens. From the time such new varieties are introduced it does take a few years for nurseries to grow these to maturity and to establish their suitability and individual requirements. In Chapter 8 about a hundred Hosta varieties are described, including some older but still good varieties; some new and some unusual varieties; and some varieties that have been raised at our own nursery. However, they are all ones that are considered to be attractive, good quality varieties which are garden-worthy, subject to any limitations for the planting positions required for that particular variety, and importantly, ones which are readily available at a reasonable and fair price from several sources. Nothing is more frustrating for the gardener than seeing a Hosta variety and being unable to obtain a plant for themselves, and nothing is more frustrating for a specialist Hosta nurseryman than to be asked for a variety which he knows is not a good grower or which is not available in this country.

CHAPTER 2

How and where do Hostas grow?

The habits of Hosta plants and their yearly life cycle from dormancy to dying back at the end of the year are described in this chapter. Furthermore there is information on how the plants are affected by cold and adverse weather conditions, by sun and shade, and by water availability, and also water retention by the plant.

Hostas are hardy herbaceous, deciduous, perennial plants. Put more simply, they are winter frost-tolerant, non-woody plants whose leaves die back in the late autumn; they complete their cycle of foliage, flowers, seed and dormancy in a year, and are able to regenerate from their rhizomes (the underground storage organs for water and plant food reserves) and roots every spring. Even if Hostas are grown in frost-free areas, they will still die back at the end of the season and go through the same annual cycle.

Hostas are best known for having spectacular foliage that, as will be seen in Chapter 3, comes in a wide variety of sizes, shapes, colours and variegation. This makes them extremely useful in the garden and containers. Their leaves are also of great value to people who make and enjoy flower arrangements in the home and elsewhere.

All the Hosta varieties should flower and whilst they are limited in the colour range, some varieties do produce spectacular flowers.

DORMANCY OF HOSTAS

Hostas are reputed to survive in winters where the air temperature falls below −20°C. At the lowest

Established Hostas in a range of varieties at Park Green Nurseries in Suffolk.

air temperatures the ground is likely to be covered with snow so that the temperature in the soil would be considerably higher due to this snow blanket and the absence of wind chill. Without the snow cover it would be a very different matter and from our experience over the years we only need to begin worrying when the night-time temperature is consistently very low and the daytime temperature remains below zero with no snow cover. The soil will retain some heat and the temperature in it will fall much more slowly than the air temperature.

Plants in containers do not get the same protection as plants in the soil and the cold can penetrate the sides of the containers and cause damage to the roots. This will be discussed in much greater detail in Chapter 5.

An internationally accepted scale of plant hardiness zones is essential to define the average winter temperatures that plants can tolerate. The United States Department of Agriculture has drawn up an American hardiness zone map and a similar one, based on the American version, has been drawn up for the United Kingdom and the rest of Europe. In these maps the zones are defined by the average annual minimum temperature for the various areas of each country as shown on the following page.

In practice this means that if a plant is labelled as being hardy down to Zone 8, then it can be expected to survive temperatures of down to −12°C.

Hostas are remarkably tolerant and adaptable plants and have been found to grow in many temperate climates. In Britain our Hardiness Zones vary from 7 in the North Highlands of Scotland to Zone 10 in some coastal areas of Southern England. It is surprising that in such relatively small countries as Britain and Ireland there are

Zone Number	Average Minimum Temperatures	
	Degrees Fahrenheit	Degrees Centigrade
Zone 1 (coldest)	Below −50	Below −46
Zone 2	−50 to −40	−46 to −40
Zone 3	−40 to −30	−40 to −34
Zone 4	−30 to −20	−34 to −29
Zone 5	−20 to −10	−29 to −23
Zone 6	−10 to +0	−23 to −18
Zone 7	+0 to +10	−18 to −12
Zone 8	+10 to +20	−12 to −7
Zone 9	+20 to +30	−7 to −1
Zone 10 (least cold)	+30 to +40	−1 to +4

Plant hardiness zones.

four different zones. Our winters can be very variable due to the influence of the Gulf Stream affecting Ireland and the West Coast of England and Scotland, which are Zone 9, and up to Zone 10 locally in coastal areas of South West Ireland, South West Devon and Cornwall, and the Isles of Scilly and the Channel Islands. Most of England, Wales and Scotland are Zone 8, while the Highlands of Scotland, the Pennines in England, and the mountainous areas of Wales are Zone 7. Some localized areas in all Zones can be in frost pockets, or sheltered areas, which can qualify them for a different Zone number. Hostas will grow well in all the Zones in the British Isles, but have a preference for areas which are cooler and wetter.

In the USA the variation is from Zone 1 in Alaska and a very small area in Minnesota adjacent to the Great Lakes, to Zone 10 in the South of the States of California, Arizona, Texas and Florida. In practice Hostas are more usually grown satisfactorily in Zone 8 down to Zone 3 but have been grown in even colder Zones. In Northern Europe there are very cold zones in Northern

Scandinavia and Russia, but our nursery has regularly sent Hostas to all these countries and the rest of Europe and elsewhere with just a few making their way to the warmer countries of Spain, Italy and Greece.

It is essential for Hostas to have a period of dormancy and cold winters are very definitely better for their growth the following season, so Hostas should never be overwintered in anything other than a cold place. It has been suggested that Hostas need to be subjected to zero temperatures for at least forty nights and experience certainly bears this out. For example, after the colder than usual winter of 2008–2009 Hostas grew very much better than in previous years. As our nursery grows many thousands of Hostas we are sometimes obliged to store dormant plants in refrigerators as there is insufficient space for them in the nursery growing areas. Plants have been kept at 0°C from dormancy in October and November to be potted up as late as the following June or July. When taken out of the refrigerator and potted these plants grow very quickly and very much more evenly than plants potted prior to the winter. Please don't try putting Hosta plants in your domestic refrigerator, because you need a commercial refrigerator with temperatures controlled to plus or minus one degree, and which are not opened every day.

Surprisingly the length of the growing season does not have a marked effect on the growth of Hostas and they grow well in countries such as Canada where the growing season is very short.

GROWTH FROM EMERGENCE TO DIE-BACK

Hostas require a moisture-retentive soil, together with regular and plentiful rainfall. Therefore, in the British Isles they perform better in the North of England, Scotland and Ireland. However, they also do very well in all other regions of Britain, even the drier areas of East Anglia.

The structure of the soil plays a very important part in determining how much moisture it can hold and this will be described in Chapter 4. Because of their root structure, Hostas are better able to withstand modest periods of drought and hot weather.

that its shape and structure can be easily seen. In the centre (the crown of the plant where the roots and shoots meet) can be seen pinkish purple buds which will produce the shoots which emerge in the following spring. These shoots arise from short rhizomes which are the storage organs of the plant, enabling the plant to regrow after dormancy.

Surrounding the central bud area is a thick mass of very fleshy roots. These also store both the plant's reserves to re-emerge in the spring and also a large quantity of water which is very quickly available to the plant when needed. The plants are best in situations where the ground can be well wetted without becoming waterlogged during the winter. This way the roots can take up all the moisture they need and surprisingly root growth does still appear to take place in the early months of winter, even when the foliage is dying back.

The early Hosta shoots are very characteristic and these open to form the leaves which gradually expand to their full size.

Hosta 'Gold Standard'. The roots, rhizomes, and buds of a five year old plant.

The early shoots of *Hosta* 'Gold Regal' – eagerly awaited every spring.

The *Hosta* 'Gold Standard' is typical for a large variety which has been grown in the garden undisturbed for about five years. The whole plant was lifted when it was dormant and then washed so

The varieties do not all emerge at the same time and there can be as much as six weeks between the emergence of the first and the last varieties. People often get worried, when some Hostas

Hosta leaves unfurling in the spring. *Hosta sieboldiana* underplanted with bluebells, and the yellow leaved *Hosta* 'Gold Haze' which must have some sun to retain the golden colour.

fail to make an appearance when expected, but they are tough plants and each variety knows its optimum time to emerge. Varieties to emerge very early include *Hostas* 'Aureomarginata' (*Montana*), 'Banana Boat', 'Big Daddy', 'Blue Arrow', 'Blue Umbrellas', 'Diana Remembered', 'Gold Haze', 'Golden Tiara' and other 'Tiara' varieties, 'Granary Gold', 'Hadspen Samphire', 'Night before Christmas', 'Sagae', *undulatas* varieties *albomarginata* and *undulata*, and 'Wolverine'.

At the very early stages of growth it is important to ensure that precautions for prevention of damage by slugs and snails are taken and recommendations for their control will be given in Chapter 7.

Given reasonable weather conditions the plants will grow quickly, but at this stage when the leaves are still very tender, damage can be caused by adverse weather conditions, particularly late snow and frosts. Fortunately there are relatively few years when this happens. Frost damage is very characteristic and in the first instance causes parts of the leaf to lose the green pigment to give almost clear windows in their leaves and their edges. These early leaves usually become covered by later emerging leaves and with luck the damage

does not show for too long. When late frosts are expected or forecast it is well worth spreading woven fleece protection over the foliage of the Hosta plants to minimize the risk and the effects of damage to the plants.

Hail can also severely damage Hosta leaves and large hailstones will penetrate even the thickest of the leaves, and can totally shred them. In the East of England this has happened twice in the last ten

A drift of *Hosta undulata* variety *albomarginata* in spring in the RHS Garden at Harlow Carr in North Yorkshire.

years or so and the damage is there to be seen for the rest of the season. It is tempting to remove the damaged leaves but it is best to leave as much of the plant's green tissue as is possible. Sometimes more leaves can be produced but in any event the plant should survive until the following year. Hail that is not heavy enough to penetrate can still leave masses of yellow or brown marks on the leaves – one for each time a frozen hailstone hits the Hosta leaves.

Hostas are typically strict clump formers and where several Hostas are planted closely they will come up individually, although at full leaf emergence it appears as a solid mass or drift.

Normally these clumps are very tight with no empty gaps in the centre, with the exception of the *Hosta plantaginea* varieties which form a ring of buds which spread outwards leaving an empty area in the centre where the plant has died out.

Not all Hostas are clump forming, and some can spread sideways through the production of 'stolons'. These are shoots formed at the base of the plant below ground level which produce a new plant at a short distance from the parent. This can form a more extensive clump which will continue

A plant of *Hosta* 'Bold Ribbons', showing a stolon which enables the variety to spread into a wide clump giving excellent ground cover.

A clump of *Hosta* 'Bold Ribbons' showing that it has been able to spread wider due to the production of stolons.

to expand until it reaches denser vegetation or is prevented by the gardener using a spade to keep the plant to size.

The smallest Hostas, likely to have first arisen at high altitudes in thin gritty soils like alpine and rockery plants, also spread quite vigorously and if left to their own devices can produce a large clump.

Small varieties like *Hosta venusta*, though low in height, are able to spread into wide clumps.

This well-established Hosta has over several years heaved itself well above the soil surface.

Hostas can be left to grow in the garden for many years, but tend to gradually shift themselves above the soil surface.

If this happens the Hosta can be lifted and replanted but it is much easier just to cover the plant with an inch or so of soil or for preference, garden compost or a similar humus-rich material.

These very young plants of *Hosta* 'June' have very narrow leaves with little variegation.

It is sometimes difficult to envisage what some Hosta varieties will look like as mature plants because the young plants often have juvenile leaves which are quite small, pointed, and narrow compared with the leaves of the mature plant. This does not occur with all varieties but it is quite marked, for example, in the 'Tardiana' Hostas.

The number of leaves that will be produced by a Hosta plant is determined by what has been initiated in the buds that will arise in the spring. This single set of leaves will subsequently emerge in the spring and remain for the course of the season. This is a great disadvantage as the Hosta is not continuously producing new leaves during the season which can replace those which have become damaged by adverse weather conditions or by pest attack. This does make it doubly important to protect the foliage from physical damage and grazing by slugs and snails. This single set of leaves generally has to last for the season. Even if the leaves are cut down during the season, the Hostas will seldom produce new foliage. These Hostas can survive until the following season but would only produce a smaller plant.

Fortunately some Hosta varieties do as a matter of course produce a single flush of new foliage in mid-summer. This is a huge advantage as the clump can be regenerated by these new leaves.

This mature *Hosta* 'June' has elegant broad leaves with wide blue margins., which makes it the United Kingdom's and America's favourite Hosta.

Hosta 'So Sweet', a fragrant flowered variety, showing fresh new growth in summer. The new leaves are smaller but with broader cream leaf margins.

In the picture two types of foliage can be clearly seen. The larger older leaves are darker with narrower variegated leaf margins. The new leaves when they first arise are smaller, a fresher green with broader creamy-yellow margins. Later in the season these will be much the same as the other older leaves.

Whatever situation Hostas are grown in, they will always die back in the autumn, when the air and ground temperature fall and when the day length and light intensity decreases. Early dormancy of plants can also be brought about by stress to the plants during the growing season. This stress can be due to excessively hot weather or severe lack of water in the soil, and under these conditions it is advisable to water the plant onto the soil and not over the foliage. If Hostas go into early dormancy, they are very unlikely to re-emerge before the following spring. With global warming we can clearly see that these values are changing and plants are growing for longer. In our garden we see that some late Hosta varieties still have green leaves in December and the buds of the earliest varieties are starting to appear in January. There are no evergreen varieties, and there are never likely to be. It is often suggested that this is a disadvantage, but overwintering leaves would look very unexciting, and every spring we have this magnificent flush of new foliage, and every year we all have an equal chance of producing wonderful, pest-free Hostas!

In a very hot year the leaves of the Hostas will start to turn brown and die back as early as September but more usually they will continue to look attractive until October or November. Varieties do not die back at the same time and in some it can be very advanced while others are still totally unchanged.

Two Hostas dying back in late autumn. *Hosta sieboldiana* variety *elegans* on the left is considerably nearer dormancy than its neighbour *Hosta* 'Margin of Error'.

The important thing is that each variety always dies back when conditions are right for that particular variety; the difference in time from the first to the last to die back is as much as six to eight weeks. This will be much the same as the time interval between the first and the last to emerge in the spring.

The weather during the growing season will always affect the performance of Hostas. There are good years and there are bad years for Hostas and the best results will always be achieved in the cooler years with higher than average rainfall.

HOSTAS AND WIND

Based quite close to the East Anglian coast, our nursery is much affected by the prevailing easterly winds at all seasons of the year. The wind affects us in three ways:

- First, if your garden is in an exposed position, plants always emerge later in the spring as the persistent winds, even slight, will cool the air and the ground surface, and hence the soil will therefore be slower to warm up in the spring. Gardeners living in more westerly and in more protected areas will always have an earlier start in the spring.
- Second, strong winds can cause damage to Hostas and other plants, and even the most robust varieties can have leaves and stems bruised and broken.
- Third, and probably the most important, the wind, particularly when it is warm in the summer, will cause Hosta leaves to lose their moisture by evaporation very much more rapidly and this can lead to the drying out and scorching of the leaves. This will be particularly marked if your Hostas are growing in too sunny a position, or during periods of intensely hot sunshine.

The best shelter from the wind is given by hedges, trees, or latticed structures, which allow the passage of some air currents, rather than solid objects such as walls and fences where strong eddies of lighter wind can be produced. Hedges, shrubs and trees will give protection immediately behind them but also some protection for a distance several times greater than the height of the hedging material.

HOSTAS IN SUN AND SHADE

Hostas do grow very well in the shade but unquestionably perform extremely satisfactorily in sun for at least a part of each day. It is always suggested that Hostas look their very best in the shade but this is because the plants will then grow larger and taller with bigger and darker leaves. In the sun Hostas will not produce such a large clump but it is likely to be more uniform, sometimes have a better leaf colour and always have more flowers. This will of course very much depend on which variety is being grown as inevitably some do better in more shade and some do better in the sun.

In the shade Hostas can tolerate quite dry soils. Gardeners will of course ask how deep the shade and how dry the soil can be. This is an impossible question to answer and the best advice is to plant an inexpensive variety or an expendable plant in that situation, keeping it well watered until established and then checking on its progress. If successful then others can be tried in the same position. If no other plants will grow in that position, it is unlikely that Hostas would be able to do so. The Hostas will grow well in indirect light but it must be sufficiently bright to enable them to carry out photosynthesis and other essential processes.

Hostas will happily tolerate some sun during the day, and the amount of sun will depend on which variety you intend to plant, because the structure as well as the appearance of varieties can be different. Water passes through plants by the process of transpiration, evaporating from the leaf surface thus cooling it and drawing up water from lower down the plant and ultimately its roots. This movement of water also enables soluble materials to be moved throughout the plant to enable it to continue growth. Should the water evaporate more quickly from the leaves than it can be taken up by the roots in sunnier and windy situations, then the leaves of the plant will be stressed and become scorched and eventually the plant will wilt; this is a natural plant defence to limit the water loss of the

Scorching of the leaf edge of *Hosta sieboldiana* variety *elegans*, growing in too much sun, too dry a soil, or both.

plant. Light scorching will first be seen at the leaf edges but this stress symptom may also be caused or encouraged by other factors, such as overfeeding.

Hosta varieties that have thicker leaves and cuticles (the waxy layer over the leaf surface) will lose water more slowly and such varieties will be better able to tolerate a sunnier situation. Other features play a part, particularly the colour of the leaf, variegation and ambient temperature. As a general rule, yellow leaves would be expected to reflect light and heat, and blue and other dark coloured leaves to absorb heat and light. One could therefore conclude that yellow Hostas are better in the sun and dark coloured Hostas best in the shade. This does not always follow and there are blue leaved varieties like *Hosta* 'Snowden' and dark leaved varieties like *Hosta* 'Devon Green' that do very well in the sun. There are also yellow and gold leaved varieties that cannot tolerate too much sun, invariably those with the thinner leaved varieties, such as *Hosta* 'Hydon Sunset'. White or cream foliage can be more sun sensitive than yellow and gold, and where a green leaved variety has a white centre or a white margin the white portion can readily scorch while the green portion remains unaffected.

Hosta varieties with particularly thin, white centred leaves such as *Hosta undulata* variety *undulata* are very prone to damage by bright sun.

Hosta 'Pizzazz'. The easily scorched creamy white edges make this variety unsuitable for a sunny spot.

Small necrotic areas will appear on the white centres and these areas can then spread over more of the white area. The centres of these necrotic areas will dry up and fall out leaving holes of various sizes. This is described as 'melting out' and the tissue killed can also be liable to attack by saprophytic fungi.

There are also white centred varieties such as *Hosta* 'Fire and Ice' which has in several gardens tolerated sun for much of the day without damage. Again the leaves of the mature variety are much thicker than the more susceptible varieties.

Some varieties, of which *Hosta* 'June' is a prime example, can show very obvious light leaf speckling or pronounced small brown dots over the leaf surface. The best explanation is that in early morning the leaves are covered with tiny drops of dew, and when the sun comes up each drop acts like a tiny magnifying glass causing the small pinpoints of scorch marks over the leaf surface.

The air temperature also has an additional effect. In countries with longer hours of sunshine and higher temperatures during the day Hostas

White leaf centres of some varieties can be easily scorched by the sun and can 'melt out' leaving brown edged holes in the leaf.

will be restricted to cooler regions at higher altitudes. Here in Britain we can get periods, generally short, of hot sunshine and high air temperature which can lead literally to the 'toasting' of leaves.

We have already established that shaded plants are taller with larger and darker leaves. Plants grown in the sun have smaller leaves but they are more numerous and can be brighter in colour. The colour and habit will therefore vary, sometimes quite markedly, according to the brightness of the light, the amount of sun or shade and the day length. It is often suggested that variegated Hostas

An established plant of *Hosta* 'Fire and Ice' with its thick leaves can tolerate a lot of sun.

A tough thick leaved Hosta variety has been 'toasted' in a spell of very hot sunshine.

are likely to lose their variegation in sun or in shade. This is not the case, but the colours and leaf shape of some varieties, particularly *Hosta* 'June', can be markedly different in sun or shade.

Hosta 'June' in the shade has broader leaves, a wider leaf margin, and is bluer and greener in colour. All of these are the plant's reaction to being in less light. The leaf is larger in order to contain more chlorophyll and the change in colour is again the result of producing more chlorophyll. This is the substance which is necessary to enable the plant to carry out photosynthesis, which is the process by which it converts water and carbon dioxide, collected from the atmosphere and the soil, into sugars, which are the building blocks for the plant's growth.

We know that plants need to have thicker leaves to be able to withstand sun, but it does not follow that all thick leaved Hostas will tolerate sun. For example, *Hosta* 'Great Expectations', which has yellow-centred leaves, will only tolerate about a couple of hours of sun during the day despite being a variety from *Hosta sieboldiana* variety *elegans* which is very considerably more sun-tolerant.

HOSTAS IN SUN AND SHADE

Such is the variation in Hostas that we cannot generalize and define the situation in which all varieties will grow best. While all varieties will tolerate and grow well in shaded conditions, they will also tolerate some sun provided there is adequate moisture in the soil. The amount of sun depends on the variety being grown. Some will tolerate only two hours or so of sun each day. The majority are happy in up to four hours a day, and others will tolerate more. Where the sun is particularly hot and where air temperatures are high, Hostas will be unable to tolerate as many hours of sunshine and this will need to be considered when Hostas are needed for planting in sunnier positions in warmer climates.

Hosta 'June' grown in the sun on the left and shade on the right, showing marked difference in the colour and shape of the leaves.

There are a considerable number of Hostas that will tolerate full sun for more than half the day, but only where there is plenty of moisture in the soil, and air temperatures are not too high. Those particularly tolerant to the sun include varieties raised from *Hosta plantaginea* marked (p), which grows in the open in the wild, and *Hosta* 'Sum and Substance' and varieties raised from it marked (s) which have leaves of particularly good substance – thick leaves with a good waxy leaf covering. Hosta varieties which can be expected to be more sun-tolerant, sheltered from wind in moist to damp soil, are as follows:

'Beauty Substance'(s)	*gracillima*	'Potomac Pride'
'Blue Angel'	'Granary Gold'	'Queen Josephine'
'Blue Mouse Ears'	'Guacamole' (p)	'Radiant Edger'
'Blue Umbrellas'	'Hadspen Samphire'	'Raspberry Sorbet'
'Chinese Sunrise'	'Halcyon'	'Rippled Honey' (p)
'Christmas Tree'	'Honeybells' (p)	'Royal Standard' (p)
'Devon Green'	'June'	'Second Wind'
'Diana Remembered'(p)	'Krossa Regal'	*sieboldiana elegans*
'Domaine de Courson'(s)	'Little Red Rooster'	'Snowden'
fortunei aureamarginata	'Little Sunspot'	'So Sweet'(p)
'Fragrant Bouquet' (p)	*minor*	'Striptease'
'Fran Godfrey'(s)	'Mrs Minky'	'Sum and Substance'(s)
'Francee'	'Niagara Falls'	*venusta*
'Gold Edger'	'One Man's Treasure'	'War Paint'
'Gold Haze'	'Paradigm'	'Whirlwind'
'Gold Standard'	*plantaginea japonica* (p)	'Yellow River'

There is one further proviso, and that is that the plant should actually emerge in the sun, and not have been recently transplanted from a position where it had more shade. When the plant emerges, it can assess the position in which it is growing and react accordingly.

In summary, the vast majority of Hostas do benefit from being in the sun for part of the day provided that there is sufficient moisture in the soil to maintain it in this position. Plants in some sun produce a better shaped clump with more leaves, better leaf colour, stronger yellows and golds and better colour contrast. They should also be less attacked by slugs and snails, which are generally confined to the shadier areas of the garden. In addition, Hostas grown in a sunnier situation will produce more flowers, which is a major consideration where flowers are the major consideration.

In practice most Hostas in the United Kingdom can be grown in a position where they are in full sun for up to half the day and shade for the other half, or in the bright dappled shade of trees, preferably under deciduous trees which will allow the soil to be fully wetted during the winter months to ensure that the soil is at its full water capacity. Should Hostas grown in these situations not perform as well as expected or exhibit scorching of the leaf centres or margins, then they should be moved at the appropriate time to a position which is less sunny or where the soil is moister. Where a garden is heavily or completely shaded Hostas are extremely useful, particularly as the choice of plants in general for these situations is more limited. Even in continuous shade Hostas still need a sufficiently good intensity of light to ensure their growth.

Where for any reason your Hosta's leaves get damaged by adverse weather, grazing by pests or any other factor, it is tempting to tidy up the plant by removing the worst leaves. Bearing in mind that the plant only produces a limited number of leaves each season, and that it relies on the green tissue to ensure its good health, the removal of leaves should be kept to an absolute minimum.

In the wild the Hosta plant is not worried about how it looks. So long as it emerges every spring to produce flowers and seeds it has fulfilled its purpose of ensuring the continuation of the species. In our gardens we expect more and in subsequent chapters advice will be given on how to keep our plants looking good, both in the garden and in containers.

CHAPTER 3

Variation between cultivars

From our fifty species in the wild we now have around 7,500 varieties and these are increasing by up two hundred or more new introductions every year. This might seem to be an enormous number but there is still room for more, and already some genera of garden plants already have tens of thousands of varieties. Hostas have a large number of significant variations so a very large number of varieties is possible. An article some years ago suggested that using every one of these variations it was theoretically possible to have over two million Hosta varieties. This could even be a conservative estimate as new varieties are being introduced which have features that are quite different from the Hostas that we are familiar with. *Hosta* 'Tattoo', with its unique maple leaf variegation, and *Hosta* 'Praying Hands', with its unusual narrow leaves and erect habit are good examples.

Most recent Hosta varieties introduced are of American origin with less than a tenth coming from Europe mainly, with a few from other countries. There are many American nurseries and gardeners who are developing new Hosta varieties and it is highly probable that we have yet to see more significant changes in Hostas that will become available for enthusiasts as well as for those who grow just a few in their gardens.

With so many varieties to choose from it is quite out of the question to collect them all. We need to be selective and grow only those varieties that we choose to grow, or to limit ourselves to collecting Hostas within a certain group, for example miniature Hostas which have become very popular.

Hosta 'Alan Titchmarsh'. A recent introduction from Park Green Nurseries. The foliage of this variety is much more striking than the flowers!

ABOVE: The unique variegation of *Hosta* 'Tattoo', but not the easiest of varieties to grow well.

BELOW: *Hosta* 'Praying Hands', despite its unusual appearance, has proved extremely popular.

About a fifth of all Hosta species and varieties are available from nurseries in the United Kingdom. This does include some which are in very limited supply, and some which are no longer popular or have very definitely been superseded by more modern and more garden-worthy plants.

Many of the new varieties are improvements on the old in terms of appearance, garden-worthiness and, dare one suggest it, pest resistance, but even so only a small proportion will become popular garden varieties. At our nursery eleven new Hosta varieties have been raised and introduced but of these only three have sold in significant quantities. Nothing is more exciting for a Hosta specialist nursery than raising new varieties, and the search is always on for promising new plants.

From choice, at our nursery we limit ourselves to selling a range of two hundred varieties and every year we replace the less popular varieties with new introductions. In this number we can have a good choice of sizes and colours without including any varieties that are too similar, and still have space for the more exciting new varieties as well as our own introductions. Of our two hundred varieties, about seventy sell really well, but as has been the case for the last twenty-five years, it is just a dozen or so varieties every year that account for the greatest portion of all Hosta plant sales.

Our most popular dozen varieties are likely to be much the same as at other United Kingdom nurseries, but we are fortunate that two varieties raised on our own nursery have proved to be among our best sellers. These are *Hostas* 'Fran Godfrey' and 'Royal Golden Jubilee', which are now available from nurseries and in countries other than our own.

As well as in the United Kingdom, *Hosta* 'June' has been the most popular variety in the United States for several years. *Hostas* 'Sagae', 'Sum and Substance' and 'Whirlwind' are among the favourite varieties on both sides of the Atlantic Ocean, but surprisingly *Hostas* 'Fire and Ice' and 'Patriot' are much less popular in the United States than in the United Kingdom.

With these statistics it can be deduced that of the many Hostas introduced, few will reach these exalted positions as it really does require an outstanding new variety to achieve this, particularly when there is such a good selection already.

Hosta Variety	Date Introduced
'June'	1991
'Fire and Ice'	1999
'Whirlwind'	1989
'Patriot'	1999
'Sagae'	1996
'Devon Green'	1987 approx
'Fire Island'	1998
'Halcyon'	Early 1970s
'Sum & Substance'	1980
'Blue Mouse Ears'	2001
'Praying Hands'	1996
'Cracker Crumbs'	2002
'Night before Christmas'	1994
'Fireworks'	2001
'Remember Me'	2001

An 'educated' interpretation of the most popular Hosta varieties in British gardens.

It is difficult to know what features determine the popularity of individual varieties because there are so many variations available. We now need to consider the more important of these variations, which include the size and shape of the plants and of the leaves and flowers, the colours, variegations and texture of the leaves, the colour, shape, time and scent of the flowers with other perhaps less prominent features.

SELECTING HOSTAS

Hostas are quite remarkable plants and can almost be tailored to any situation and to individual requirements for size, habit and colour. In selecting Hostas for any planting situation you can just choose the variety that appeals to you the most! Alternatively, it can be done more logically by first considering the size of plant required. Should you have a small garden or a small space available, then it would be unwise to plant varieties that are known to develop into very large plants. Conversely it would also take a very large number of small varieties to fill a large space. The size categories given for the varieties are a very reliable indication of the sizes that they will achieve in the garden. Generally the medium and large varieties are the most popular and within these categories there is an extremely good choice.

Careful consideration needs to be given to the inclusion of small and very small varieties as these have shallower root systems and will need to be planted into soils that are not likely to dry out. Additionally many of the very small species and varieties originate from species that grow in thin, well-drained soils and therefore they do not like soils that are too wet. For these reasons they are best suited to being grown in containers, where the moisture and nutrient content of the soil can be carefully controlled.

Where there is a large area to be planted with Hostas, the most satisfactory results are achieved using a range of different-sized varieties so that the plants do not all finish up at the same height.

The next major consideration is the planting situation. The effect of exposure to wind and sun has already been considered, and should plants be intended for these situations it is necessary to use varieties with thicker leaves that are less likely to lose too much moisture by evaporation. Where plants are to be grown in sunnier positions this will influence the choice of varieties; suitable ones were listed in Chapter 2.

Pests and diseases are the subject of Chapter 7 but at this time it should be mentioned that if slug and snail populations are likely to be high, then it would be wise to choose varieties that have a more erect habit, and also thicker, firmer leaves which are less palatable to slugs.

After these considerations, it becomes largely a matter of personal choice. Individual tastes vary enormously, but there is always a strong preference for varieties with good leaf variegation,

and these varieties always dominate the lists of popular varieties. There is a very good selection of colours – gold, yellow, cream, white, green and blue – and variegation – marginal, central streaked and others. Sometimes there is a preference for single coloured non-variegated varieties. Here there is the same selection of colours, and the choice of this may be more strongly influenced by the texture and finish of the leaves which may be flat and shiny, cupped, wavy edged, undulating or twisted. Blue-leaved varieties are always very popular as so few other hardy, temperate plants can produce as good a quality blue as Hostas. Some of the ornamental grasses can do it, but very few other plants. Hostas can offer a range of colour shades and with blues, for example, these can be dark, light, silvery or greenish blue. The gold and yellow varieties tend to be the least popular as this colour is sometimes associated with plants that are sickly or suffering from a trace element deficiency.

Where larger groups of Hostas are being grown it is always best to have a mix of some single-coloured leaved varieties with the variegated varieties for a better effect. The alternative is to have a drift of several plants of the same variety. It is also necessary to decide on the leaf colours of adjacent Hosta plants where there is the choice of using contrasting colours such as yellow and blue together or the use of co-ordinating colours where varieties of different shades and variegations of the same colours are used.

Finally, there are the flowers, which may be the overriding consideration. For example there are varieties with pure white flowers, and white beds can be a big attraction. There are also some varieties with scented flowers, and scented beds can again be a big attraction.

SIZE AND HABIT OF HOSTA PLANTS

It is only possible to give a guide to the size to which Hostas can be expected to grow and many different versions are used to classify this. Our nursery uses the following categories to describe the plant size at three to five years after planting

Size description	Approximate Size of Plant Clumps 3 to 5 years after planting	
	Height in inches (cm)	Width in inches (cm)
Very small	Under 6 (15)	4-10 (10-25)
Small	6-10 (15-25)	6-12 (15-30)
Medium	12-15 (30-40)	18-24 (45-60)
Large	18-24 (45-60)	30-36 (75-90)
Very large	Over 24 (Over 60)	Over 36 (Over 90)

With their wide variation in size, Hosta varieties need to be sorted into an understandable classification.

one of our typical young plants (usually single divisions, sometimes more, particularly with small varieties at the point of sale).

This system allows us to judge which size category each Hosta variety falls into, and also to be able to classify a variety in an intermediate category, for example, Small to Medium, if it does not clearly fit into either category. In this way we

A clear indication of the variation in Hosta variety sizes. A small variety, *Hosta* 'Golden Tiara' in the right foreground, a medium variety , *Hosta* 'Eric Smith' to its left, and a large variety, *Hosta* 'Gold Regal' in the right background.

are able to give a realistic comparative size for the varieties.

It always has to be borne in mind that the actual size may not be the same as the guide figures. In the shade the plants will grow taller and wider, and the same will apply if they are grown in very fertile or well-fertilized soil. The plants will be smaller if grown in soil which is not so moisture-retentive, or where they are subject to continued pest attack.

In this picture there is a clear size difference although the age of the three main plants is the same at about five to six years. The green and yellow variegated plant in the right foreground is *Hosta* 'Golden Tiara' and this is a small variety. The blue green plant in the left foreground is *Hosta* 'Eric Smith' and is a medium variety, whilst the green-gold leaved plant in the right background is *Hosta* 'Gold Regal' and is a large variety. At this stage each plant clearly fits into the allocated category and whatever situation the plants are grown in, they cannot change sizes!

We also have very small varieties and pictured below is Hosta 'Cat's Eye'.

This is a plant two years on from a small division and it is still little bigger than its 9cm pot.

The American Hosta Society have clear criteria for classification of Miniature varieties. They state that the leaf blade area must be no greater than about $4in^2$ ($26cm^2$) and the leaf blade without the stem must be no greater than about $4\frac{1}{2}in$ (11cm) long. The 'about' is to allow slight leeway in borderline cases. The measurements must be of a mature leaf and not include the leaf stalk.

A miniature, *Hosta* 'Cat's Eye' which remains very low but will spread to make a neat wider cushion.

At the other end of the spectrum are the very large varieties, with some classified as Giants. Some Hostas such as 'Sum and Substance' can reach huge proportions, and mature plants can reach a diameter of over 9ft (2.7m) from a single division, over a period of several years

A five year old *Hosta* 'Sum and Substance' at the start of its journey to be part of a show display.

Hosta 'Krossa Regal', a classic example of an erect vase-shaped clump.

Hostas can be left to grow undisturbed for many years without being divided, and they generally form tight, well-filled, uniform clumps. This happens particularly when they have been left undivided for several years, and where there is not too much competition from surrounding plants. Some varieties produce compact lower clumps whereas other varieties produce very erect growth giving elegant vase-shaped plants that stand out well in the garden.

A few varieties, as we have seen earlier, are able to spread but still maintain a tight, though non-uniform, clump.

Every year it is exciting to see the Hostas emerge after their winter dormancy. At this stage can be seen the first example of variation in the genus with marked colour differences in the new shoots and some, particularly varieties from *Hosta plantaginea*, where the buds are much less tightly packed.

The colour of the buds is often totally unrelated to the colour of the emerged foliage but the variety can be recognized by an enthusiast from the bud colour.

Different colours of the early shoots are displayed by the strong red shoots of *Hosta undulata* variety *undulata* top left, the more muted tones of *Hosta* 'Snowden' top right, the plain green shoots of *Hosta* 'Pizzazz' bottom left, and the purplish shoots of *Hosta* 'Rhapsody'.

There is an huge difference in leaf size between the enormous *Hosta* 'Sum and Substance' with a leaf 14 inches (36cm) wide and 16 inches (41cm) long and the tiny *Hosta* 'Cat's Eye'.

THE FOLIAGE OF HOSTAS

This is the subject of the greatest relevance and also the greatest amount of variation. We have to consider the size, shape, and finish of the leaves; their colour and whether they fade or change colour; whether they are variegated and the type of variegation; the nature of the leaf surface and margins; and the shape and colour of the petioles (leaf stalks).

The size and shape of leaves

As there are very large differences in the size of plants so there are also very large differences in the size of individual leaves. It does not necessarily follow that the largest plants have the largest leaves or the smallest plants have the smallest leaves though it is usual that they do. Sometimes small or medium-sized varieties have disproportionately large or small leaves.

The leaves of Hostas are always simple, in that the edges are never serrated like nettle leaves nor of complex shapes and finely divided like maples or ferns. The leaves of Hostas can be smooth and flat like *Hosta* 'Devon Green' or strongly puckered like *Hostas sieboldiana* or 'Good as Gold', or they can be cupped like *Hosta* 'Abiqua Drinking Gourd'. The edges of the leaves can be slightly rippled like *Hostas* 'Crested Surf' and 'Rippled Honey', strongly undulating like *Hostas undulata* variety *undulata* and 'Hadspen Samphire' or crimped like *Hosta* 'Embroidery'. The blade of the leaf is most usually flat but can be twisted like *Hosta* 'Whirlwind'. The leaves can be anything from round or heart-shaped to very narrow and lance-shaped like *Hosta* 'Fireworks', or even more extreme like the species *Hosta longissima*, which has very long and narrow leaves as the name implies. Additionally the leaf surfaces can be shiny, dull, or glaucous, and are not necessarily the same on the upper and lower surfaces.

Single colour leaves – the beautiful blue of *Hosta* 'Halcyon', the gold of *Hosta* 'Eric's Gold', the dark green of *Hosta* 'Devon Green', and the sage green of *Hosta* 'Snowden'.

The colour of leaves

Leaf colour in Hostas is undoubtedly their greatest attraction, whether in single colours or in two or more colours in the variegated varieties. The colours found in the foliage can be white or cream to nearly silver, yellow or gold, blue and pale to deep green and almost black. All shades and tints of these colours can be found in illustrations throughout this book. Quite a number of very dark green Hostas are being introduced with names like 'Black

OPPOSITE PAGE: Foliage in its many forms – puckered, undulating, cupped, smooth, flat, shiny, dull or glaucous, heart shaped or elongated, rippled, crimped or twisted.

Beauty', 'Black Pearl', 'Lakeside Black Satin', 'Lakeside Coal Miner' and 'Sea Ebony'. All are described as having dark green foliage, but grown in the shade and in the right growing medium can produce these extremely dark and almost black leaves. The variety names are very often a strong indication of the varieties' major characteristics and plenty use words such as Blue, Gold, Green, Red, White Edge, Piecrust, Wrinkled, Crinkled, Ruffled, Giant, Large, Big, Baby, Tot, to name but a few!

The non-variegated yellow and gold coloured varieties can change quite markedly and generally fall into one of two categories. First those which emerge yellow and gold but which then fade through chartreuse to green. Some like *Hosta*

Hosta 'White Feather' which emerges with all white leaves, but these soon start to turn green.

fortunei variety *albopicta* form *aurea* do this within a period of only a few weeks while others like *Hostas* 'Gold Haze' and 'Granary Gold' will do it more slowly, but if kept in a sunny position will hold the colour better and even be bleached lighter in more sun. Where the colour change is from yellow or white to green this is termed viridescence. Other yellow and gold leaved varieties like *Hostas* 'August Moon', 'Piedmont Gold' and 'Zounds' will emerge green but as the light intensity and day length increase will brighten to yellow or gold and as long as they get enough sun during the day will hold the colour until the end of the season. The sun is absolutely essential for the best colours in these varieties. Where the colour change is from green to yellow or gold, this is termed lutescence.

The blue leaved varieties are always among the most popular Hostas. When they first emerge the colours can be rather disappointing as they are sometimes more green than blue, but as they develop the blue colour becomes much more pronounced. The best blue is always found in the more mature clumps; it is given by a 'bloom' or a waxy powdery coating on the leaf rather than the colour of the leaf itself and the word used to describe this is glaucous. If one of these leaves is rubbed part of the blue covering will be removed to leave a dark green streak. These blue leaves can be disfigured slightly by water marks, particularly if watered from above with hard water, when the lime in the water can be deposited on the leaves. This is because when the water lands on these waxy leaves it will leave large droplets which will not run off as they would on a smooth leaved variety. As the water in the droplets evaporates it leaves any soluble chemical deposited in that position. For this reason blue leaved Hostas are particularly susceptible to being marked by debris falling from the trees that shade them.

Much publicity has been given to the all white *Hosta* 'White Feather'. No plant can exist for long with only white because they have no chlorophyll and are unable to carry out photosynthesis, which enables the plant to live. White seedlings occur on occasion but seldom, if ever, survive. In the case of 'White Feather', it starts after two to three weeks to green up along the veins and this will continue until the leaf is completely green.

It is worth mentioning that in autumn Hostas can add to the autumn colour by producing very attractive golden leaves.

Hosta leaf stalks (petioles) are usually shades of green, whilst some variegated varieties have striped stalks, for example green and white, and quite a number have red stems. This includes, for example, a variety named *Hosta* 'Regal Rhubarb', and to answer the obvious question, yes, the Japanese did, and possibly still do, eat Hostas. By all accounts the taste is not impressive! In some new varieties the red speckling from the leaf stalks has reached the leaves and it is almost certain that, with continued selection of the plants with the most red on their leaves, it will be possible to produce a red leaved variety. Considerable progress has already been made in this direction.

Hosta 'Halcyon' whose normally blue leaves have changed to a stunning gold in the autumn.

Hosta 'One Man's Treasure' – shiny dark green leaves, with deep red markings stretching from the petioles onto the leaf.

Note also the shape of the leaf channel and the cross section shape of the petiole (leaf stem) is an important diagnostic feature for Hostas. The petiole channelling very neatly diverts rainwater and condensation to run from the leaf blade down to the base of the plant where it is needed.

The colours found in the single colour leaves are also found in the leaves of variegated varieties in a combination of two or more of the colours, many examples of which are illustrated throughout this book.

The phenomenon of variegation is caused by mutation of individual plant cells usually in the meristematic tissues of the tips of the plants buds. The margin colour of the variegated leaves arises from a different layer of these tissues. Generally these mutations occur from natural causes but it is possible that accidental damage to the meristematic tissues can cause such changes. Such damage can be deliberately inflicted on the plants, through X-rays or chemical treatment for example, to bring about changes and encourage the formation of variegated varieties.

There are different forms of variegation, the more usual being where the paler colour is on the margins of the leaf – termed marginal variegation, or where the paler colour is in the centre of the leaf – termed centre or medio-variegation. There are several variations on this theme, where the central colour is surrounded by a different shade of that colour or by a different colour. There can be streaking of the colours, often to the centre of the leaf, together with other effects. Additionally, the widths of the variegated margins or centres vary. Sometimes, a narrow leaf margin can be just as effective as a broad one.

Hosta 'Fire Island'. One of the most popular more recently introduced varieties. Yellow green leaves tinged with red at their base.

Variegated Hostas. The cream margined 'Barbara Ann', the broad gold margins streaked to the leaf centre of 'Carnival', the white centred 'Night before Christmas', and 'Striptease' with the pale gold leaf centre margined in white.

Variegated varieties can also have leaves that are streaked, mottled, splashed or have other irregular types of markings. Generally these types of variegation are less stable and very variable. When these varieties are propagated by conventional division or by the laboratory technique of tissue culture or micropropagation, results can be extremely variable and there can be a very high failure rate. It can be fairly said that with variegations of these types no two leaves are ever the same.

For a number of reasons the leaf colours and shades can vary. We have already seen how they can be affected by the proportion and the intensity of sun and shade.

The leaf colours can also be affected by the maturity of the variety where generally the colour improves with age. Soil fertility and the balance of nutrients and chemical trace elements can also have an influence. They can also be affected by the seasonal maturity and newly emerged plants very often look a relatively poor colour, but this will improve as the season progresses. In many of the Hostas with white variegation this may at early emergence look distinctly yellow but will change as the season progresses through cream to white. This is termed albescence. Certain varieties can change quite radically during the season. Probably the best known and most obvious is *Hosta fortunei* variety *albopicta*, which in the early part of the season has bright golden leaf centres and dark

Hostas with unusual variegation. The white streaked leaves of 'Spilt Milk', and the green splashed creamy yellow centre of 'Revolution'.

green margins, but within a few weeks this will change to shades of green and subsequently to plain green.

Some other varieties go through these changes and lose their variegation. There is absolutely no way that this can be prevented, although a sunnier situation may extend the variegation for a very short while. Every year, however, they will go through these same changes and will always be at their peak in the early weeks of the year. The vast majority of variegated varieties will not be affected

in this way and their colours will be distinct during the season; it must never be assumed that these varieties will lose their variegation.

Variegated Hostas are less competitive than their single coloured, particularly green, relatives. If a variegated Hosta throws up plain green leaves they will be much stronger and will in time smother the variegated leaves. It is essential therefore, that these plain leaves should be cut off as soon as convenient and certainly before they get a hold in the plant.

Fran Godfrey, the BBC Radio 2 presenter, with her Hosta, grown in the shade. A young plant of the same variety grown in the sun, is very different in appearance.

Hosta fortunei variety *albopicta* has bright golden leaves in May, but the colour changes to shades of green over the next few weeks.

THE FLOWERS OF HOSTAS

All of the Hosta varieties will produce flowers. Occasionally these flowers are sterile and will not produce viable seeds. Hostas grow quite slowly from seed and are unlikely to produce flowers until their second or third season. Often, young Hosta divisions will flower in their first season but are more likely to produce them in their second season. This varies with different varieties.

Although Hostas are not usually grown for their flowers, it is a welcome addition, and should they fail to flower this can cause disappointment. Plants will always flower best when they are growing in the sun or bright dappled shade. Should they be growing in a very fertile soil, they may produce abundant, very healthy foliage but no flowers. Plants always tend to flower better when growing conditions are against them and in these situations it is a natural reaction for the plant to flower and produce seed to ensure continuation of the species. Occasionally a nutrient imbalance in the soil may prevent them from flowering and a potash-rich fertilizer as used for roses may encourage the production of flowers.

Hosta flowers are produced on stems, termed scapes, which arise from the base of the plant.

The scapes are simple stems occasionally branched and are usually very strongly upright as illustrated, but they may also be curved and leaning. At the top of the scapes are the flowers; botanically the arrangement of the flowers is called

Flowers of *Hosta* 'Gold Regal' at their best, just as the lower petals are beginning to shrivel.

a raceme, as each individual flower is attached to the scape by a short stem, the pedicel. At the base of each pedicel is a leaf-like structure or bract, which varies in size from quite insignificant to large, according to the variety. In some varieties further bracts can be found further down the scape and can be clearly seen in the last illustration. These bracts lower down the scape may be quite large and leaf-like and are usually the same colour as the foliage on the rest of the plant. The bracts at the base of the pedicels will wither when individual flowers die back and set seed.

The flowers making up each raceme may be dense as in the last illustration or may be more widely spaced as in the scented flowering *Hosta plantaginea* and its offspring. The individual flowers last only a short while and then wither and die.

Flowers open in order from the base of the raceme. Unfortunately the lowest flowers are usually shedding their petals and setting seed well before the flower buds at the top of the raceme begin to open. Once the petals start to drop they can stick to the upper leaves and ultimately they start to develop fungal rots, which can spread to the leaves. In other varieties the petals shrivel and remain attached to the developing seed pods. If you do not want to wait until all the flower buds open, it is better to remove the flower stems when the petals begin to fall and the plants will then look much neater. It is best to cut back the scape to just below the level of the foliage canopy, leaving the larger bracts. If the flowers are not wanted there is the temptation to cut them off at a much earlier stage, but sometimes they will then regrow.

HOSTA FLOWERS

While the colour range of the flowers is somewhat limited to shades of white, lilac, lavender and purple, nevertheless they are a pleasant addition to the foliage for which they are best known. These colours can vary slightly according to the climate of the country in which they are grown. In sunny positions Hostas will produce more flowers and a massed group of Hostas in flower can look spectacular, particularly if there is a range of flower colours.

Hostas are in flower at different times of the year according to variety, with some flowering as early as May and others as late as October. The majority will flower between June and August. The flowers do not appeal to everyone and they can be cut down and removed when the petals of the lowest flowers on the stem start to drop. It is not advisable to cut them down too early as the plants have a marked tendency to send up more flower stems.

All Hosta blooms are like small lily flowers and apart from their colour do not vary significantly in their shape or structure. However, there are differences in the size of the flowers and their density on the stems, and there are varieties that are able to produce scented flowers.

Illustrations through this book show that there are varieties of Hosta with very attractive flowers, but the greatest interest is in the flowers which are white, and which are scented, and preferably both! *Hosta plantaginea* has comparatively large, pure white, strongly scented flowers. There are over sixty varieties from this Hosta species, but not all of them have pure white flowers; some are not as strongly scented; and some are quite small plants. Hosta 'Snow Flake' for example has pure white, slightly scented flowers, but in full flower only stands just over 1ft (30cm) tall. However, a few of these varieties do have the bonus of double-petalled flowers, though this advantage can be outweighed by the relative difficulty in getting these varieties to flower well.

Hosta plantaginea has remained popular because with its large white flowers it is frequently used in borders that have all, or the majority of, flowers in white with plain green leaves. There are however, many other white flowered varieties with both single colour and variegated leaves to suit all preferences.

When removing Hosta flowers cut the stalks to below the level of the top of the leaf canopy.

The structure of the flowers

Hostas were once included in the Lily family and have flowers, which, although smaller than many lilies, have much the same flower arrangements, with six of each of the main floral components, except for the single central female structure.

This flower has six petals which are fused further down forming a tube with the ovary at the base. There are also six stamens, each consisting of a filament with the brown anther at the tip. The anthers produce yellow powdery pollen which can be clearly seen in the illustration. The pollen contains

A typical Hosta flower showing its six petals, six stamens bearing pollen producing anthers, and the single white female pistil.

the male chromosomes. Each flower contains a single white pistil – the female component, which in the illustration is to the left of the stamens. This consists of a long style which is hollow and ends at the front with the stigma which is the receptive female tip, and the ovary at the base of the flower.

In the process of pollination, generally by winged insects, pollen is transferred from the anthers to the style and fertilization of the ovules within the ovary is achieved. Individual flowers can be self-pollinated; that is they are fertilized by pollen which they produced, or cross pollinated when the pollen is carried to another flower on the same plant or on a different plant.

Variation in flowers and flowering

Hosta varieties do not all flower at the same time. The form used for the International Registration of Hosta Cultivars divides flowering times into five distinct periods:

1. Before 1 June
2. June to mid-July
3. Mid-July to mid-August
4. Mid August to the end of September
5. After 1 October

It is remarkable that Hostas are able to flower over such an extended period. Generally the scented flowering varieties are among the last to flower, but *Hosta tardiflora* can still have flowers emerging in November. This time scale is intended for use on a global scale and in the United Kingdom the majority of varieties fall into the middle three categories. The months have to be changed for growers in the Southern Hemisphere.

The shape of flowers does not differ substantially but there are three recognized types.

The most usual are described as tubular, as found in *Hosta* 'Ginko Craig' and its sport *Hosta* 'Sarah Kennedy' illustrated above, with more extreme forms being described as spider shaped as found in *Hosta* 'Lily Pad', and they can also be bell shaped, as found in an as yet to be named sport

Flower shapes do not differ very significantly. From the top tubular, spider and bell shaped.

The impressive large double, pure white, very fragrant flowers of *Hosta* 'White Fairy'.

of *Hosta* 'Blue Angel'. There are also a limited number of Hosta varieties with double flowers.

These double flowers are quite spectacular particularly when they are also scented – which they are as these varieties are from *Hosta plantaginea*. Probably only three of these varieties are available in Britain. These are *Hosta* 'Aphrodite', which typically has ten to twenty petals in place of the usual six, and was first described in China as early as 1940. *Hosta* 'Yu Lei' was imported again from China in the late 1990s when it was renamed *Hosta* 'White Fairy' on its arrival in England (it is closely related to *Hosta* 'Aphrodite' but with a slightly different flower arrangement). *Hosta* 'Venus' is a 1993 sport from *Hosta* 'Aphrodite' but with up to thirty petals on each flower. These three varieties all have the usual pure white, strongly scented flowers. Unfortunately it is not always easy to get these varieties to actually produce flowers in the British Isles. Usually the varieties grow well to produce big plants with healthy foliage but not a flower to be seen. These probably will only flower

south of a line from the Bristol Channel in the West, and The Wash in the East. Because these varieties flower so late in the season, they need to be in growth for longer. This means growing them in containers, giving them the required period of dormancy and starting them into growth in early February in a warm and bright greenhouse or conservatory. Once the risk of frost is past the containers need to be placed in the garden in a sheltered sunny position. It is also essential that these and other *Hosta plantaginea* varieties are kept very well watered particularly in July and August, or grown in a soil which is continually moist to damp, as is the case in the country of origin of this species.

The most obvious difference between flowers is the colour of their petals, which can vary through shades of white, lilac, lavender and purple. On a global basis the colours for individual varieties can vary with temperature, brightness of the light and day length. In practice many Hosta flowers are a shade or two darker in the British Isles and Europe than those of the same variety grown in the

Hosta flowers. Pure white 'Snowden', purple 'Tambourine', white, tinged pale lavender 'Blue Umbrellas', and striped flowers of 'Tea at Bettys'.

United States. In Britain there can also be seasonal differences in the colour of flowers.

The pictures show a selection of flower colours starting with the pure white flowers of *Hosta* 'Snowden' to the purple flowers of *Hosta* 'Tambourine'. Really pure white flowers are not common, and many varieties have flowers which can best be described as off white, like *Hosta* 'Blue Umbrellas' which has white flowers with a very

pale lilac tinge. Many varieties have striped flowers like *Hosta* 'Tea at Bettys' and many also have translucent edges to the petals.

The size of the flowers varies with variety, usually in proportion to the size of the plant, but the largest flowers again come with *Hosta plantaginea* and varieties raised from it. This variety is well known for the scent of its flowers – a strong sweet perfume that can be detected from several yards away.

The bright red flower stems of *Hosta* 'Cherry Berry'. These bear deep purple flowers.

As with the stems of the leaves we also get some colour variation with the flower stems. Most varieties are shades of green to white but some are more strongly coloured, for example the very dark, almost black stems of *Hosta* 'Little Black Scape', but some are red and probably the most remarkable is *Hosta* 'Cherry Berry'.

Pollination and seed set

When the flowers have died, and provided that pollination has taken place, the fertilized ovary will develop into three chambered pods containing the ripening seed. Once this is mature the seed pod will split open into three sections and the seed, in two rows in each section, will be shed and fall to the ground, though being winged they can be carried modest distances by the wind. Not a very sophisticated method of seed dispersal but nevertheless one that has ensured the survival of Hostas over many centuries. Under British conditions the seed does not readily germinate naturally, but in Holland, where the soil is very moist, the seed germinates much more readily and becomes a serious nuisance. In this instance the removal of the flower scape prior to ripening will prevent the emergence of these unwanted seedlings.

Just one more variation: the ripening pods show a marked difference between varieties and we have a nice range of colours from white through green to red and purple.

Other diagnostic features are used to differentiate species and cultivars and these include scape length, structure of the anthers, the prominence of leaf veins, and others only of real interest to the pure botanists!

Shiny black seeds of *Hosta sieboldiana*. Each is nearly ½in (1cm) long. Smaller varieties produce proportionately smaller seeds.

A selection of Hosta seed pods in differing colours and sizes.

CHAPTER 4

Hostas in the garden

A Chelsea Show garden featuring foliage colours with Hostas in the foreground.

WHY GROW HOSTAS?

Hostas are ideally suited to growing in gardens in temperate climates, preferably where there is regular and plentiful rainfall. Although there are significant differences in the amount of rainfall throughout the British Isles, Hostas will grow well in all regions but do have a preference for the wetter areas in Scotland and the North of England, Wales and Ireland. Hostas

A simple courtyard garden for easy maintenance with plants in shades of green and white. *Hosta* 'Patriot' in the foreground with *Hosta* 'Francee' near the pool.

are adaptable plants, which tolerate wide-ranging conditions and there is a good choice of Hostas to suit individual preferences. They also have other advantages which ensure their popularity as garden plants.

Hostas – the foliage plant

Many gardeners are making increasing use of foliage to provide continuity of interest in the garden over the growing season. In gardens, and particularly at the garden shows, we are becoming increasingly used to seeing gardens almost entirely based on foliage, with few or no flowers.

The co-ordinating foliage colours of *Hosta* 'So Sweet', grasses, and ferns, with yellow flowered perennials.

Hosta 'Twilight' with the foliage of ferns, maple and willow.

The flowers of most perennial plants do not last for long, perhaps just a very few weeks, and inevitably during spring, summer and autumn there are periods when there are few in flower. At these times foliage can be used to provide colour, impact and continuity. Foliage comes in practically all the colours needed, and Hostas with their range of leaf colour, habit and texture are a popular choice.

With foliage as with flowers we have the choice of co-ordinating or contrasting colours. In this picture the foliage colours co-ordinate perfectly, and the contrast is in the shape and texture of the foliage. The variegated *Hosta* 'So Sweet' with its broad leaves is very similar in colour to the grass which has very simple long narrow leaves. Grasses and Hostas, because of their contrasting leaf shapes and their very similar spectrum of leaf colours, are ideal companion plants. The colour of the Hosta also tones very well with the fern and again there is a strong contrast between the simple Hosta leaves and the strongly divided leaves of ferns. Because of their preference for similar planting situations ferns are again ideal companion plants. Also included in the picture above are yellow flowered *Achillea* and other perennials. Again, these are in colours which co-ordinate beautifully with the foliage colours,

although contrasting colours can also be very effective. The same co-ordinating effects can easily be obtained with other foliage colours.

Many other perennial plants can be used with Hostas to give good contrasts in foliage such as *Astilbes, Epimediums, Polygonatums, Rodgersias, Rheums,* and others that have similar requirements to Hostas.

Hostas can of course be grown in beds on their own, though most people would prefer other plants to be grown with them to emphasize their size, to provide a textural contrast, to give more height and to give added interest. Where Hostas are grown in groups of different varieties, considerable care needs to be taken over the choice of sizes and foliage colours. The most pleasing results are achieved where there is a mixture of plant sizes with the use of co-ordinated colours in the adjacent Hosta plants. While it is tempting to use strongly contrasting colours such as blue and gold this does not often give good results. It is particularly difficult to place varieties with strong

An impressive *Hosta* 'Frances Williams' surrounded by the foliage of ferns and grasses.

white variegation in a group of Hostas as one's eye will immediately be drawn to the strong white element of the group. It is preferable to grow the green and white varieties together using as contrast the different heights, sizes, leaf shapes and type of variegation. Better still to use these white variegated varieties in all-white borders or white sections of the garden, as these are very popular in larger compartmentalized gardens and provide a very relaxed feel, yet providing strong impact.

The stunning foliage of *Hosta* 'Patriot' in bright shade.

Where a large selection of variegated Hostas is being grown together, the inclusion of some varieties with single coloured leaves is advisable. Too much variegation gives a very confused and over fussy result. The more brightly coloured Hostas are also very useful for brightening up dull areas in the garden, and this is where the white variegated Hostas can be particularly useful.

The foliage colours of Hostas can also be used to co-ordinate or contrast with the colours of the hard landscaping. Bright warm gold and yellow Hosta foliage goes well with woodwork, brickwork and gravel, whereas the cool blue colours go well where slate paving is used in the garden. Dark foliage can also be used to give a strong contrast with pale limestone stoneware.

Hosta 'Gold Standard' lightening a dark corner of the Beth Chatto Gardens in Essex.

FOLIAGE PLANTS FOR THE GARDEN

Hostas are almost certainly the most popular foliage perennial in the garden in temperate countries, and while they can offer a good range of colours they cannot cover the whole spectrum. Gardeners wanting to use more colours in the garden can obtain plants that are able to provide the remaining colours as well as totally different foliage textures. Looking first at grass and grass-like plants, these come in much the same colour range as Hostas but can also provide black foliage as in *Ophiopogon planiscapus* 'Black Dragon', and red as in *Imperata cylindrical* 'Red Baron'. Some varieties of *Panicum* and *Miscanthus* have foliage in shades of red and purple, while nice shades of bronze and glossy brown are found in species of *Carex*. Ferns as well as their intricate foliage can provide more exotic colours than shades of green. For example *Dryopteris erythrosora* has foliage in a nice shade of orange, while the *Athyriums* have silver leaved varieties; meanwhile others, like the variety 'Red Beauty', have silver foliage and purplish red in the area of the leaf veins.

Other perennials include some species and varieties with a spectacular range of foliage colours. To choose a few, the *Heucheras* offer a foliage colour range from green through shades of yellows and golds to reds and purples. Silver foliage is also found in *Lamiums* and *Pulmonarias*, and in total contrast purples in differing shades are found in varieties of *Ajuga*, *Bergenia*, *Ligularia*, *Persicaria* and *Rheum*. Some of these can be found with quite intricate variegated foliage.

Seasonal variations also produce foliage colour in perennials, such as the red in the spring foliage of some *Epimediums* and the autumn and winter colours to be found in many genera, species and varieties. The colours found in herbaceous perennials are more than matched by the foliage colours of many of our hardy trees and shrubs. It is hardly surprising that foliage colour has become such an integral part of our gardens.

Hostas for long term growth and low maintenance

Hostas do not mature fully for about three to five years after planting out as young plants. However the great advantage is that they can be left for long periods of time to produce good mature, established clumps. Such older plants have uniform clumps with the best quality foliage, and which provide the greatest impact in the garden. In our nursery we have demonstration borders with spectacular Hostas that were planted over twenty years ago. There are records of Hostas being left undisturbed in the soil for over seventy-five years.

It is always assumed and indeed recommended by many authors and media presenters that Hostas must be divided every three years or so to keep them to a reasonable size and to freshen them up. This is certainly not so and it is a fairer representation to say that if Hostas are treated in this way and divided every three years they will never make good specimen plants. Nowadays it is not unusual to see mature Hostas which have obviously been growing in the same position for ten years or so, and which look simply magnificent. The frontispiece of this book shows a group of Hostas which have been growing together in the same position for about eight years and which are very much approaching their peak. Some perhaps are a little tightly packed but it is infinitely better to have total cover of the soil surface.

The argument that Hostas must be constantly divided to keep them to a reasonable size is seldom tenable. Guidance is given on the size that a Hosta is expected to reach under average conditions three to five years after planting. In practice, even after a few years more the plants have not grown appreciably larger. By that time the size of the Hostas is not influenced so much by their age, as by the climatic conditions during that particular season. In a cool, damp year they will grow larger that in a hot dry year. To illustrate the size differences here are the measurements of some varieties after three to five years and again after a further ten years.

A choice of Hostas to complement or contrast with various types of hard landscaping.

Plant size	Hosta variety	Width of clump in inches (cm) after	
		3–5 years	10–15 years
Very large varieties	'Blue Umbrellas'	40 (100)	56 (140)
	'Paul's Glory'	42 (105)	56 (140)
	'Snowden'	42 (105)	60 (150)
	'Sum and Substance'	48 (120)	84 (210)
Large varieties	'Gold Haze'	40 (100)	54 (135)
	'Striptease'	40 (100)	48 (120)
Medium varieties	'Devon Green'	24 (60)	34 (85)
	'Fire and Ice'	22 (55)	26 (65)
	'Halcyon'	27 (65)	42 (105)
	'June'	28 (70)	42 (105)
	'Nicola'	22 (55)	32 (80)
	'Wide Brim'	24 (60)	36 (90)
Small Variety	*venusta*	14 (35)	32 (80)

Comparative sizes of Hosta varieties when semi-mature and fully mature.

The *Hosta* 'Sum and Substance' described here did, in an exceptionally mild and wet year, reach a diameter of 9½ft (290cm). The *Hosta venusta* showed a comparatively large increase but the small varieties are known to spread into quite wide clumps. The sizes quoted in this table will be regarded by some as rather small, but these Hostas have received only light applications of organic fertilizers, and are growing in one of the driest areas of England, where the average rainfall is just over 20in (50cm) each year.

The figures quoted are slightly misleading as the semi-mature plants had unrestricted space, but the mature plants were partly limited by surrounding vegetation as would be normal in most garden situations. However, these figures do indicate that the Hostas do not spread as quickly after they have reached semi-maturity at three to five years. This is not unexpected as the size is determined by the diameter of the bud area, and the growth of plants in general is limited to a maximum for each species and variety. Most plants, particularly trees, have a predetermined maximum size.

Well-established clumps of Hostas with their broad leaves are excellent as ground-cover plants. Before planting anything it is essential to remove the roots and stolons of all perennial weeds as few cultivated plants are able to compete with them. Hostas can very successfully shade out annual weeds and very few would be able to grow up through the dense Hosta foliage. So long as the entire soil surface is kept covered by the Hosta foliage very little maintenance of that area would be necessary. This complete ground cover can be achieved by planting a mixture of Hosta varieties or Hostas with other good ground cover plants or a drift of Hostas of the same variety. Where using a drift or making a larger clump of the same variety it is always best to plant in odd numbers as even numbers will usually give too geometric a group.

ABOVE: A mature clump of the very large *Hosta* 'Krossa Regal' – left to mature in the same position for several years.

BELOW: Hostas for ground cover. On the left a group of different varieties, and on the right a drift of the blue-veined *Hosta* 'Halcyon'.

HOW TO USE HOSTAS

Sun and shade in the garden

Previous chapters have described the climatic conditions that best suit the growth of Hostas. While some varieties can grow well in more sun, the vast majority grow best where they are shaded for at least half the day. The shade need not necessarily be given by tall trees or large buildings. Lightly-shaded positions can easily be achieved by the use of shrubs, taller perennials, low walls, fences, and artificial structures such as pergolas and arbours. Since the sun moves round during the course of the day, such plants and features can be used to provide shade for a certain portion of the day.

When shaded, it is important that the Hostas are still in bright light or dappled shade where possible in order to maintain their colour and uniformity. They can tolerate deeper shade but lack of sufficient light will cause the plants to become drawn out and to produce softer growth. The best shade is supplied by smaller trees and by taller tree canopies which do not have dense foliage. Generally Hostas are much less successful underneath or nearby evergreen trees as the soil and plants will be continually sheltered from the rain resulting in very dry soil conditions. Conifers are particularly unsuitable as their fibrous roots will remove the majority of moisture from the soil.

The most suitable trees to shelter Hostas include maples, flowering cherries, apples, rowans and some larger trees such as oak. Certain trees, particularly willows and beeches, grow surface roots which will take up all available moisture and also make it that much harder to cultivate the soil and plant the Hostas. As trees grow, their lower branches should be periodically removed to ensure that sufficient light can reach the Hostas growing underneath them. Care must always be taken when planting trees in the garden to ensure that they will not grow too large and cast too much shade over the garden. Advice should also be taken to ensure that they are not planted too close to any buildings, where they could cause structural damage.

When Hostas are growing in the shade it is best to avoid those tree species and varieties that shed a profusion of flower petals, seeds and other plant debris which can stick to the Hosta foliage and spoil their appearance. A particular problem occurs where trees provide roosting sites for larger birds, especially pigeons. Bird droppings on the foliage are not a pretty sight.

Apart from preventing too much exposure of Hostas to the sun, the shade is also important for protection from the wind, and because the shade improves the microclimate and the amount of moisture in the soil. In the shade it will be cooler and moister and less water will evaporate from the plants and from the soil surface.

Planting positions for Hostas

Provided the amount of shade is satisfactory and that soil conditions are suitable, as described later in this chapter, then Hostas can be grown in many situations in the garden.

Hostas can be used in garden borders of all types – with other herbaceous perennials, in shrub borders and in mixed borders. They look most effective as large specimen plants to give impact and to provide a focal point in the border. Sufficient space needs to be allowed for them to reach full size, and to give emphasis to this, they are best underplanted with low growing ground-cover perennials. Their relatively low spreading mounds of bold foliage are particularly effective when they are grouped with taller plants with a strong vertical habit. They can also be spaced to provide breaks in long borders. They mix quite naturally with flowering perennials and with other predominantly foliage perennials, and are suited to growing in both formal and informal garden designs.

Hostas always look at their best by water and somehow that is a situation where they are always expected to be found. In our Hosta displays at the garden and flower shows, water is always included as it shows the plants to their best advantage. Natural ponds and streams do ensure plenty of moisture in the surrounding soil but Hostas are

Examples of different ways to use Hostas in the garden – in borders, as edging, by water, with flowering plants, in gravel and so on. Top left is in the Beth Chatto Gardens, and top right in East Ruston Old Vicarage Gardens.

not naturally bog plants and their roots have not evolved for growing in waterlogged soils. Hostas do not like to grow in the water as marginal plants although occasionally this has been seen. If water levels fluctuate Hostas can survive immersion for short periods, and if dormant can survive with water covering their planting positions for several weeks and even the duration of the dormant season.

Hostas can be used in gravel gardens, with stones, and the smaller varieties may also be included in rockeries. It is always rewarding to grow Hostas to maturity where there is no competition from surrounding plants, and this can be achieved by allowing them plenty of space and growing them in beds covered with gravel to give a good cover to the soil. A lower density of plants would be grown in this way but they can be allowed to grow to their full size. The gravel cover is an excellent mulching material, easy to tidy and which keeps down annual weeds, ensuring that the soil surface is cool and moist. It is a mild deterrent

against slugs and snails, and additionally it cannot be blown away like lighter materials; nor can it be worked down into the soil by earthworms.

Hostas are also grown as edging plants in more formal settings. Small Hostas may be grown individually or in a continuous line around beds, and by the side of paths, patios and other hard landscaping to soften the hard and straight edges of the stone or brick work.

It is perhaps unfortunate that, in common with many other perennials, the foliage of Hostas dies back in later autumn to leave bare ground in the winter. However this does provide an opportunity to underplant the Hostas with late autumn and early flowering spring bulbs such as *Cyclamen hederifolium,* winter aconites, snowdrops, early crocuses, and *Narcissi.* As the Hosta foliage emerges it will progressively cover the dying foliage of the bulbs. Later in the season Hostas may still be interplanted with bulbs such as *Alliums* and taller lilies.

Hostas bordering paths and pools. The pale yellow green *Hosta* 'Gold Regal' and the variegated *Hosta fortunei* variety *albopicta.*

Hosta 'Francee' planted with *Alliums*.

HOSTAS AND THE SOIL

Our gardening activities are governed to a great extent by the type or types of soil we have in our garden. The soil type may prevent us from growing some plant varieties, though sometimes it is possible to improve the soil and to adjust in a small way problems such as soil acidity and alkalinity, moisture retention, or drainage. More usually, the properties of the soil cannot be changed in a season though long-term treatment can result in a significant improvement.

Soil types and classification

In the same way that Hostas are dependent on adequate daylight, air and water, they are equally dependent on the nature of the soil in which they are to be grown. Soils vary throughout Britain and other countries and there can be very marked differences within short distances. Soils are produced by the very gradual breakdown of rocks from erosion and from weathering, both brought about by wind, water, high and low temperatures, and by chemical and biological processes. This includes colonization by plants whose roots aid the breakdown into soil particles and encourage the passage of air and water. During these various processes the particles become progressively smaller until they form soil, which is made up not only of this mineral material from the originating rocks, but also organic material, air and water. The proportions of each of these constituents are of great importance in the performance of these soils in producing vegetation.

The mineral content of the soil determines its texture as this is controlled by the particle diameter sizes in the soil as follows:

- Clay particles   0.002mm or smaller
- Silt particles   0.002 to 0.05mm
- Sand particles   0.05 to 1.0mm
- Gravel   1.0 to 32.0mm

Most soils are a mixture of all these particle sizes and the proportions of each determine the performance of the soil. Soils with a high proportion of clay particles are the most moisture-retentive and usually the most fertile, whereas soils with a high proportion of the coarse sand particles are the freest draining and the least fertile. A perfect loam soil will contain a roughly equal mix of clay, silt, and sand particles to give good drainage and reasonable fertility and which is easy to cultivate at most times of the year.

Where soil is derived from chalk, a very soft rock, it is generally of poor quality as such soils are often shallow and stony. It can be soft and sticky in periods of wetter weather, and is also highly alkaline, which will not permit the growth of acid-loving plants.

The content of organic matter also affects the soil greatly. This organic matter, usually called humus, is the decomposed remains mainly of plants, but also of other organisms, including invertebrates, birds and animals. Soils with a very high organic content are found as peaty soils, which occur for example in the Fens of East Anglia. Peat itself results from the decomposition of sphagnum moss, or grass and sedge, in marshland and bogs. High levels of organic material give rise to more acidic soils which are not suitable for plants which require alkaline conditions.

The acidity or alkalinity of soils is defined by the pH scale which runs from 1 for strong acids, to 14 for strong alkaline materials, with neutral – neither acid nor alkaline at pH7. Soil testing kits can be easily purchased to check the pH of your soil, though the types of plants growing in the garden would be a good indication, with *Calluna*s, *Camellias,* and *Rhododendrons* requiring the more acid soils. *Hydrangeas* can be useful in giving an indication of soil pH as their flowers are predominantly blue on acid soils and pink or red on alkaline soils. In practice soil pH is unlikely to vary more than from pH4 to pH8, and nutrients will become less available to the plants in soils of high or low pH. Plant growth is generally best between pH6.3 and 6.8. In the more acid soils micro-organisms are less active and from between pH4 and pH5 earthworms will no longer be present in the soil. Hostas are remarkably tolerant of a wide range of soil pH but have a preference for the more acid conditions found when there is a high proportion of organic material in the soil. They are, however, able to grow in alkaline chalky conditions provided there is an adequate depth of soil. Hostas can also tolerate growing in coastal areas where there can be a higher salt concentration in the air, leading to a higher concentration in the soil. Areas which have been flooded with sea water would be unsuitable for Hostas until soil conditions have stabilized.

GARDEN SOILS

Depending on the size of the mineral particles and the humus (organic material) content, our garden soils can be divided into several descriptive categories:

- **Loam** – the ideal soil, an equal mixture of clay, loam and silt particles.
- **Clay loam** – a mixture of more of the fine clay particles with loam. This would be more moisture retentive than loam alone.
- **Sandy loam** – Loam in a mixture with coarse sand, which would be freer draining than loam.
- **Clay** – a heavy soil which can be difficult to manage. However, it is the most fertile and the most moisture retentive. People are fond of complaining about clay soils, but these, correctly managed, grow the best crops, and permit the growing of a very wide range of plant varieties. Hostas do very well in these soils.
- **Sandy clay** – clay in a mixture with sand so more free draining than clay and easier to manage.
- **Sand** – a light coarse soil generally in a mixture with some clay or silt particles. This is a very acidic free draining soil which is easy to cultivate at any time of year but which is very prone to drought, and is low in fertility.
- **Chalky soils** – thin white alkaline soils which become very sticky in wet weather, and dry in warmer weather.
- **Peaty soils** – Very dark acidic soils which hold moisture very well but can become boggy as they do not drain well. They are very fertile and the addition of lime will help to reduce their acidity.

By the soil colour and by rubbing moist soil between the fingers it is quite easy to estimate the main particle size content. A sandy soil will feel gritty, a moistened clay soil will readily produce a polish when rubbed and a silt soil will feel soapy or greasy.

There are intermediates between the categories listed above. All soils, except peat, will benefit from the generous incorporation of organic material. Clays and loams make excellent garden soils and are the more usual. Soils with a high peat or silt content are uncommon and are restricted to specific local areas.

Free draining soils will be less fertile as soluble nutrients are more easily dissolved and washed through the soil (leaching). Soils therefore which hold the moisture better will also usually be the more fertile.

Soil Improvement

The structure of the soil is as important as its constituents. It is necessary to have a crumbly, friable soil which is neither compacted, nor where a hard layer or 'pan' has formed a few inches down, which can prevent root growth deeper into the soil and which will also prevent adequate drainage of the soil. Good soil structure is indicated by good plant growth, a good even mid-brown soil colour, a sweet smell and plenty of earthworm activity.

The greatest improvement in garden soils is brought about by increasing the humus content of the soil by the incorporation of organic material such as well rotted animal manure, leaf mould, garden compost, spent mushroom compost, green manures, plant by-products such as spent hops, straw, bark, sawdust, and similar materials. It is important that the materials are well rotted or composted, because if incorporated into the soil

An attractive mix of Hostas with other foliage plants contrasting in colour and texture.

Raised Hosta demonstration beds at Park Green Nurseries in Suffolk.

while rotting they can produce excessive heat, as well as containing a much higher content of viable weed seeds. Uncomposted materials, due to bacterial action, can reduce nitrogen levels in the soil and cause plants to become yellow and reduce their growth. The addition of organic material is mainly to increase the moisture holding capacity of the soil but it also provides plant nutrients and on heavier soils it improves drainage and aeration. The organic material should be added when the soil is moist and warm.

Good drainage is also essential because in a wet soil water replaces the air in the pores in the soil, which becomes stagnant due to an adverse effect on the beneficial bacteria in the soil. Air in the soil is essential for good root growth, except in plants that have specifically evolved to grow in waterlogged soils, which do not contain any oxygen.

Hostas are not, contrary to popular belief, plants which will happily tolerate these conditions. Some varieties are known to grow in very wet soils, but generally Hostas need to grow in well drained but moisture retentive soils.

When soils are very wet drainage pipes may sometimes need to be installed, but in less extreme conditions cultivation of the soil and the incorporation of organic or sandy materials will assist with soil drainage.

On very poor or very wet soils the use of raised beds can produce improved results. Soil levels can be raised, preferably with the use of retaining walls of brick, stone or wood, and a better quality soil can be used with the addition of plenty of humus to give a very much-improved planting medium. Some watering may be necessary as the soil in raised beds is likely to dry out more quickly.

Planting Hostas

Hostas are at their best on medium loam soils to heavy clay soils, and in practice such soils will contain sufficient moisture to support Hostas growing in situations from continual shade to half the day in full sun. The need for incorporating humus into the soil cannot be over-emphasized, because this organic material will enable the soil to hold moisture yet make it more open to assist the movement of air and water.

Hostas can be grown on lighter sandy and chalky soils, provided they contain plenty of humus, and provided that humus is applied to the soil surface every year for as long as possible, as this will continually build up the humus levels in the soil. Sandy soils are the most prone to drying out and plants may need to be watered particularly during periods of hot and windy weather.

Before planting Hostas the soil should be well cultivated, preferably by digging and at the same time incorporating organic material. Digging will break up any compacted soil and gives the opportunity for removing the roots of perennial weeds. All soil cultivation is best done when the soil is neither too wet nor too dry. Invariably this means that autumn and spring are the best times. Heavy soils, in particular, are best dug in the autumn, left to weather during the winter, and planted up in the following spring.

Hostas can be planted at almost any time of the year but it is best to avoid periods of very hot weather, usually late July and August, or the very cold weather in January. Plants received as a bare root with no soil or compost should be planted with the absolute minimum of delay. If weather or soil conditions are unsuitable the bare root plants should be temporarily potted in compost and planted in the garden when conditions improve. There are advantages to planting in the autumn when the soil is warm and moist and when there is time for the plants to grow and settle in before becoming dormant. Planting in the spring is also perfectly satisfactory as the worst of the cold weather will be over and the plants will quickly start to come into growth. At this time of the year the soil will be much colder than in the autumn and it is advisable to delay planting if the soil is also still very wet.

Dig out a generous planting hole for the Hosta plant. If this is a medium to large variety make the hole at least 18in (45cm) wide and 12in (30cm) deep, and larger if the soil has not been recently cultivated. Fork over the base of the hole to ensure that there is no soil compaction and incorporate some well rotted manure or other organic material. The soil removed from the planting hole should be mixed in equal quantities with some good friable organic material such as garden compost or leaf mould. If planting a containerized Hosta, take it out of the pot and remove surplus compost by teasing out the roots, particularly where they are dense, to ensure that the plant will grow away more quickly. Plant it in the soil keeping the level the same as it was in the pot. With bare root plants spread out the roots and plant so that the buds (assuming that the plant is dormant) are about an inch (2.5cm) below the soil surface. If the bare root plant is growing place it in the soil so that the fresh clean part of the plant is above the soil level as it is likely to have been before lifting from its compost. Fill in the planting hole, now containing the Hosta, with the mixture of soil and organic material, frequently firming this soil until it is full and level with the surrounding soil.

With a good, well-prepared soil containing plenty of organic material there is no need for the application of any additional fertilizer at this stage. If it is believed to be necessary fertilizer can be applied once the Hosta has made sufficient growth. What is important at this stage is to apply mulch over the soil surface around the plant. This will help to retain moisture in the soil and provide further plant nutrients. Mulches are important and will be described in detail later in the chapter. Whatever the time of year, the newly planted Hostas should be well watered with about half a gallon (3-5 litres) of water, and particularly in the spring and summer this will need to be repeated at regular intervals for about four weeks.

Particular care needs to be taken when planting small Hostas as they need a well-drained soil and will not thrive in overly wet soil conditions. The very small or miniature Hostas are shallow rooted and more prone to rotting, so are much better suited to being grown in containers or raised beds. When applying mulches around the smaller

A mulch of chipped bark round the small *Hosta* variety 'Golden Tiara'.

varieties it is important that the mulching material does not cover the central area of the plant. A thin mulch of grit or gravel around the small varieties is usually best to ensure good water drainage at the soil surface.

Transplanting Hostas

Transplanting can be carried out at the same times recommended for planting. However, if the plant is actively growing at the time of transplanting, the foliage almost certainly will be damaged and it may be necessary to cut this back. This is best kept to a minimum because the early removal of any green tissue capable of photosynthesis will slightly debilitate the plant.

When lifting a Hosta for transplanting the use of a garden fork is preferable to a spade as this will result in less root damage. However, to lift a large well-established specimen, the use of a spade is unavoidable, but there will be considerable damage to the roots. The Hosta may be transplanted as an entire plant or it may be divided at this time. Division will be described in Chapter 6, but at this stage it is recommended that the plant is divided after lifting rather than in the ground. Once it is lifted the plant can be divided cleanly with a sharp large knife or a garden saw. Clean, neat cuts are much preferred to hacking at the plant with a spade or axe. Sometimes this is inevitable and it is amazing that the Hosta can

Hostas really do mix well with practically all styles of planting, even in the most informal settings.

survive this, although the individual divisions will take longer to produce good plants. If a part of the Hosta is to be replanted in the same position it is essential that the planting hole is refreshed by thorough cultivation and the incorporation of plenty of organic material. After planting in this position, generous watering is necessary until the plant is growing well without the need of further attention.

HOSTA CARE THROUGH THE YEAR

Winter is the time of least activity in the garden, and so it is the natural start to the yearly requirements of the Hostas. It is advisable to apply a layer of organic material over the Hostas before the worst of the winter to give them extra protection from extreme cold. The earthworms will work this compost down into the soil and improve its structure. Prolonged sub-zero temperatures, when there is no snow cover, can also cause drying out of the soil and could lead to dehydration of the Hosta roots. Under these circumstances it may be necessary to check whether the ground needs to be watered.

The application of mulch to the soil surface is as important as the incorporation of organic material before or at planting. The mulch must be applied when the soil is still moist, and if possible still warm, and this is best done for convenience in the late autumn to early winter or early spring before the Hostas have started to emerge. The materials used for mulching can be the same as those used for incorporating in the soil or maybe other, totally different materials. What is most important is to cover the soil surface with a material which keeps the soil surface cooler and reduces the water loss from the soil surface. To achieve this, whatever material is used, it must be applied thickly enough over the soil surface. Where an organic material, such as well-rotted animal manure, garden compost or leaf mould is used, it needs to be about 2in (50mm) thick. Where a harder material, such as bark chippings, grit or gravel is used, this needs to be about an inch (25mm) thick. These latter materials will be particularly useful as they look attractive and they will suppress the emergence of annual weeds, whereas the organic mulches may themselves contain some weed seeds. These hard mulches can be doubly useful as a deterrent to slugs and snails – this will be fully described in

The Hosta in the right centre combines well with this very bright, mixed planting of herbaceous perennials.

Chapter 7, and it must be remembered that any programme for the control of slugs and snails must be started just before these creatures emerge from their overwintered eggs, or from hibernation.

In the early spring it is necessary to consider what additional nutrients, in the form of fertilizers or plant feeds, will need to be applied to the plants or to the soil before Hosta emergence. In the wild Hostas rely on whatever nutrients are available in the soil or whatever lands on them from above in the rain and plant or animal debris from trees growing overhead. Wild Hostas will only grow where these nutrients are available in suitable form and quantity to ensure their growth and survival. In the garden we are asking the plants to accept the position we have given them, but we want them to look that bit better than those plants growing in the wild.

Hostas will respond to applications of fertilizers, but too much will lead to excessive growth of the plants which will become soft and make them more liable to damage from late frosts, late snow, wind, hail and sun, particularly in more open positions. As with vegetables, the use of high rates of fertilizer will increase plant yields but reduce their quality. Foliage that is too well fertilized will also be much more attractive to their predators, particularly slugs and snails. Providing that we are growing our Hostas in a good soil with plenty of organic material incorporated this will be rich in nutrients, which will be topped up by the nutrients in organic mulches. The organic materials we are using as mulches (or to incorporate into the soil) do have very variable, often unbalanced, and sometimes surprisingly low levels of the nutrients required by plants.

Plants have complex requirements for nutrients. The three major nutrients are nitrogen, phosphorus (phosphate), and potassium (potash). nitrogen is the major nutrient for growth, the building block for protein production in the plant, and which is most responsible for the rich green colour of the foliage. Phosphorus is of major importance for root growth, and potassium is required for the production, size and quality of flowers and fruits. For example, rose and tomato fertilizers contain high levels of nitrogen and potassium. Plants also require other nutrients notably magnesium, calcium and sulphur and a number of trace elements in smaller amounts. Deficiency of any of these can cause adverse effects in plants but are less likely in plants grown in the garden than in containers. Information will be given on container growing in Chapter 5.

For Hostas in the garden an application of a natural organic all-purpose fertilizer such as bonemeal, or fish blood and bone fertilizer, applied in late February, and lightly raked into the soil is convenient and generally sufficient. The action of these fertilizers is slow but long lasting. Their activity is dependent on temperature, and some gardeners therefore prefer the use of soluble synthetic fertilizers which may be applied later. The rates of use quoted in the directions for use of the fertilizers are usually over generous, so a rate reduced by up to 50 per cent is often appropriate. It is very definitely best to avoid any high nitrogen fertilizer such as Growmore, pelleted chicken manure and others. These are generally intended for purposes other than feeding Hostas and other herbaceous perennial plants. Care must be taken with chicken manures as they take longer to compost. If applied before they are fully matured they can be too 'hot' for the plant and cause scorching.

The Hostas are well worth watching as they emerge in the early spring for the structure and the colours of the emerging buds. It is important to check that the plant buds are not struggling to emerge through an over-zealous application of mulch or thick weeds. A close watch is necessary for any signs of attack by slugs, snails or other pests as damage caused to the emerging buds can be visible for a considerable time. Some growers advocate the application of liquid fertilizers at this stage but this is not necessary if a natural organic fertilizer has been used earlier. Liquid fertilizers release their nutrients much more quickly, as unlike natural organic fertilizers they are not reliant on microbial activity in the soil. An alternative to liquid fertilizers is to apply synthetic slow- or controlled-release fertilizer granules which are usually formulated to contain the appropriate concentrations of all the chemical elements required by the plant. These granular fertilizers can be applied shortly before or at the time of Hosta emergence.

A stunning group of *Hosta* 'Regal Splendor'.

In the early spring it may be necessary to cover plants with a suitable fleece material; this ensures protection against a possible late night frost which could damage the emerging Hosta foliage. It is best not to leave the fleece on during the day as it could make the atmosphere around the covered plants too wet and this could lead to rotting of the foliage.

Hosta plants are best divided in the autumn or in the early spring when the buds are just visible, and full information on the division of Hostas is given in Chapter 6. As detailed earlier, Hostas can emerge over a period of up to six to eight weeks and the time for division will vary accordingly. If your Hostas have still not emerged after this time, it is worth investigating below the soil surface to see if there is still a viable plant. If not, then this is a good time to plant a replacement. However if there is the risk of a virus infection (see Chapter 7), it is vital that another Hosta is not planted in that position for several weeks.

From the time the Hostas are expanding their leaves it is important to check that the soil remains moist. This is a word open to misinterpretation as some gardeners equate moist with damp, which is in fact a lot wetter than moist! If plants are not developing well by this time of the year, either the temperature is unseasonably low or the soil is too dry. Developing Hostas use a lot of water and the growth of the foliage starts before the growth of the roots, particularly with newly planted young Hostas, and they will sometimes need further watering until the foliage is fully developed. Once this is done, the plants will quickly develop new roots which will improve the uptake of water. Where plants are watered from above it is best not to do this when the sun is shining directly onto them. Watering should be done at cooler times of the day, preferably in the early morning so that the leaves can dry before the sun is on them, or late afternoon towards early evening after the heat of the day. With the later watering there is a risk of the damp attracting slugs and snails.

On lighter soils or in drier locations the installation of a simple irrigation system will very much improve the performance of your Hostas. One of the best systems is the use of 'trickle hoses' which can be permanently located in your borders and controlled by hand, by time switches or by computer. When connected to a water supply the water trickles very slowly from the porous hose and keeps the soil moist.

Trickle irrigation. This provides even widespread watering of borders.

Such trickle pipes should be on the soil surface under the mulch and will then be at their most effective and also not visible in the border. The soil surface should not be flooded as this can lead to the soil surface becoming 'puddled' and impermeable, resulting in the water running off and not being absorbed into the soil. Overwatering must be avoided as this will lead to the soil becoming waterlogged and unsuitable for the growth of Hostas. Watering onto the ground below the Hosta plants is always preferable to watering from above, as drops of water left on the leaves can lead to damage when exposed to bright sun. This is particularly so on glaucous-leaved Hosta varieties, where drops of water may leave deposits on the foliage, particularly when the water contains high levels of lime as found in hard water areas. It is not advisable to let Hostas become too dependent on artificially applied water as it is never the same as a good spell of heavy rainfall. Hostas too used to artificial watering will tend to produce more roots just below the surface of the soil when they need to be encouraged to drive their roots into the lower levels of the soil to find moisture.

From the early spring, and throughout the flowering season weeds need to be kept under control. While Hostas are good ground-cover plants that compete well with germinating weeds, soil cover is not achieved until the Hosta leaves are fully expanded. It is therefore sometimes necessary to hoe during the early spring and summer to keep these weeds under control.

During the summer the growth and condition should be watched, particularly for pest damage and any signs of virus infections (described in Chapter 7). The condition of the leaves should be checked: if any wilting or flaccidity is seen, keep the plants watered; if any unexpected yellowing of foliage is seen, the use of a plant tonic or all purpose plant food (at half the recommended rate) may improve the condition of the plant; if the plant is getting unnecessarily scorched, try to move it to a shadier or moister position. Should a plant for no obvious reason be performing less well than in previous years and it will not respond to watering, it may be wise to lift it and plant it in a container to keep a closer watch on it. In these situations, low soil moisture is the most likely problem and the application of a plant tonic or pick-me-up could then do more harm than good. Instances do occur where in the middle of a group of very healthy Hostas, one previously healthy plant will fail to emerge or struggle unsuccessfully. Sometimes this cannot be explained, and it is just one of those things which happen! Even when we cannot explain it, remember that the plant is always right.

As summer is gradually replaced by autumn the Hostas will start to become dormant. The plants become less turgid, their leaf colours will gradually fade and become yellowed. If you want to relocate any of your Hostas this is the time to transplant them or mark their position for moving them when their foliage is gone. As the day length shortens and the temperature drops, the foliage will start to die back. Usually frost will hasten this, and it is a good idea to remove the leaves once they can easily be pulled away from the plant. If the dead foliage is left on the ground it provides a safe haven for slugs and snails to conceal themselves and lay their eggs in the ground below the dead leaves. Young slugs and snails emerging in the spring are in a prime position for a juicy meal! After the removal of the dead Hosta foliage the borders can be tidied up and levelled before the winter mulching.

A foliage display with Hostas predominating in a garden water feature.

CHAPTER 5

Hostas in containers

Hostas are excellent plants for containers, and are probably the most popular foliage perennial for this purpose. Many gardeners with high slug and snail populations have found that their only way to grow Hostas with reasonable success is to resort to having them in containers. At this stage it is fair to say that this will give some measure of protection, but on its own this is not enough to ensure that the plants grow without any damage. Other measures are also necessary, primarily the choice of a suitable position for the container, but additional precautions and measures for slug and snail control may be necessary and these will be fully described in Chapter 7.

When growing Hostas in containers it has been found that they grow extremely well and can produce some quite spectacular results, especially if they have sufficient space and have few or no plants around them. It also avoids damage from slugs and snails. This alone justifies the growing of Hostas in containers with the reduced slug and snail damage as a bonus!

The positioning of Hostas in relation to sun and shade was described in the last chapter and the recommendations apply equally to Hostas grown in containers. Once again, we need to site our Hostas in their containers in bright shade to sun for up to half the day, bearing in mind that some Hosta varieties will, in a moist soil, tolerate greater amounts of sun.

Gardeners still ask if Hostas can be grown in containers, and it is necessary to ask ourselves what it is that they need from the medium in which

Hostas 'June', 'Striptease', and an unnamed variety grown from seed giving a welcome display by a garden entrance.

they are growing. Basically, this is anchorage and support, water, and nutrients for growth. These can be provided equally well by growing Hostas in containers, but the big difference is that when they are grown in containers we have to supply all the needs of the plants ourselves. In the garden the soil can provide virtually all these requirements with very little attention from gardeners. This chapter will cover all we need to do to provide the Hostas' needs when they are grown in containers.

WHY GROW PLANTS IN CONTAINERS?

The most obvious reason for growing plants in containers is to have vegetation, either decorative or productive, where there is no soil available in which to grow them. This could be where there is no garden at all, but where there are areas of available pavement, paths, patios, or balconies where plant containers can be situated. It could also be in gardens where there are hard-standing areas needing plants to provide interest.

Containers can be used for growing tender plants that need to be moved to a frost-free place in the winter. If the garden soil is neutral or alkaline containers can be used for plants that require special soil types, such as those which will only grow in acid soils.

Among the many plants which adapt well to growing in containers, Hostas are outstanding, but grow better where particular attention is paid to their particular requirements. Many gardeners grow them by treating them like any other potted plant, but there is always a better way to achieve the very best results.

WHERE TO PLACE HOSTA CONTAINERS

A well decorated doorway or house entrance is always much more inviting and it is an ideal setting to show your prize Hostas in containers. This can be a formal arrangement in containers as shown in the picture below or it can be an informal grouping of several plants in containers.

Hostas can be used in a wide range of other containers to decorate the walls and windows of houses. There are many types of containers for attachment to the walls, for hanging containers, and for window boxes. Hostas have proved suitable for all of these.

Hostas in containers are also useful to provide interest in paved and gravelled areas where they soften the regular edges and pattern of the hard landscaping.

When Hostas have been planted in containers, this considerably adds to the height of the plant, which is useful in areas of low plantings and where greater impact may be needed.

Sometimes when there is a shortage of flowers

Two *Hosta sieboldiana* variety *elegans* in containers make an imposing house entrance at East Ruston Old Vicarage Gardens.

An informal group of Hostas in containers at a house entrance.

Two plants of *Hosta* 'Halcyon' making an attractive window box.

Hostas 'Diana Remembered' and 'So Sweet' give added interest to a formal paved area.

Hosta 'Night before Christmas' in a plastic-lined basket brightens up a dark garden corner.

A mature potted *Hosta fortunei* variety *aureamarginata* provides height and interest.

An impressive display of potted Hostas in a well staged group.

or other colour in the garden, borders may need something to brighten them up again and Hostas in containers strategically placed in a border can provide this colour together with a contrasting leaf texture can give the necessary impact.

The great advantage of Hostas and other plants in containers is that they can be easily moved until the best arrangement is achieved, or if at any time they are not at their best, they can be put somewhere out of the way until they are suitable

The bright foliage of a young *Hosta* 'Fran Godfrey' livens up a bed of hardy Geraniums after they have finished flowering.

Three show displays by Park Green Nurseries using Hosta varieties in baskets and wooden planters.

to use again. This is particularly useful when containerized plants are grown in groups. It is one of the best reasons for planting Hostas in containers since placed in groups the individual pots can be moved until the best arrangement is found. It is also possible to vary the heights of some of the containers by placing them on bricks or pieces of wood to achieve the best effect. Changes can be made during the year according to the individual Hosta's seasonal variation. These groups can be of Hostas alone or with other foliage and flowering plants.

It is important to vary the height of the Hostas in the containers to achieve the maximum impact of the group. The Floral displays at the Flower and Garden Shows are simply arrangements of containerized plants, placed to achieve the most attractive results. Sometimes the plants are presented in attractive containers and sometimes the space between the plants is filled in, and covered with fresh moss.

CHOICE OF CONTAINERS

Gardeners are fortunate that they are spoilt for choice of containers available at garden centres and at the flower and garden shows. Before choosing a container, there are a number of basic considerations. When growing plants in containers, it is the plants we want to see rather than its container. If we do see the container it is important that it is not too bright a colour, particularly one that clashes with the colour of the Hosta. Also the container should not be so over ornate as to detract from the Hosta it contains. With the range of coloured containers available it is usually possible to find a plain or simple patterned container whose colour will co-ordinate nicely with the major colour of the Hosta. Trial and error with various colours and patterns will invariably give the best result. Very often the use of inexpensive plastic pots in a neutral colour will give a very satisfactory result.

There are practical considerations in the choice of the container's shape. Very narrow container bases can be a disadvantage if there is any likelihood of the container being blown over by the

Examples of tapered pots suitable for Hostas and other containerized hardy perennials.

wind or in well-frequented places where people or traffic are likely to knock it over. Generally it is better to make use of broader-based containers. It is also wise to use tapered containers for Hostas or other long-term perennial plants. These will need to be re-potted from time to time and the plants can be extracted very much more easily from a tapered round pot rather than a straight-edged or square pot. Anyone who has grown Hostas or other perennial plants, particularly *Agapanthus* varieties in globe shaped containers will know that it is either necessary to break the pot to save the plant or reduce the plant to tiny pieces to save the pot. If you leave it long enough, the plant will make the decision and break the pot for you!

The very shallow containers that were popular in the 1950s are best avoided as the compost will dry out very much more quickly than deeper containers of the same volume. The only exception to this would be growing very small Hostas, which are best suited to shallow soils and pots.

Several types of materials are generally used for the manufacture of plant containers. These include clay (terracotta), plastic, stone, wood and metal. All of these can be used but clay pots are preferable. The clay is porous so that water will be drawn into it from the compost and will soak through the pot to evaporate from its outer surface. This will cool the pot and in turn keep the Hosta roots cool. This does suit the Hostas but nevertheless they will grow very well in black plastic containers, which will not allow the passage of water and will absorb the heat of the sun. Glazed clay pots will also be unable to benefit from water evaporation from their surface

A terracotta pot which has been badly damaged by exposure to hard frosts.

but the thickness of the pot will help to keep the roots cool, particularly if unglazed on the inside.

Clay pots will vary in their resistance to frost. By their nature, clay pots will absorb water and in the event of a hard frost followed by a quick thaw, some will flake or crack due to the expansion of ice within the clay.

Nowadays many clay flowerpots are guaranteed to be frost proof; they are fired at a high temperature over several days. Unglazed clay pots come in a vast range of styles and sizes and the plain, machine-made clay pots represent very good value for money. The ones made by hand are of course rather more expensive. When new, the colour of clay pots is quite bright, but with use they will weather well to give a more natural look. Glazed clay pots come in even greater variety, are generally less susceptible to frost damage and can be purchased incredibly cheaply as the result of imports from other countries, particularly the Far East. Clay pots do not have an unlimited shelf life as they can be quite easily broken, but because of their suitability for Hostas, the choice of pots, range of styles and sizes, and cost, they are ideal.

Wooden containers are very good for Hostas. Wood is an inexpensive and easy material to work with and if treated with a suitable paint or preservative, will last for several years. Wood is particularly good for troughs and windows boxes, which can be made to measure.

Glazed and unglazed pots in a variety of styles, colours and shapes.

Metal containers for Hostas make a welcome change from more conventional materials.

Plastic containers are inexpensive and are virtually indestructible until they become brittle after many years usage. They are used commercially because they are light, stack compactly, and are relatively inexpensive. For the gardener they are available in many shapes, colours and sizes. As they are lightweight they can be less stable than heavier materials but in neutral, unobtrusive colours they serve very well for Hostas.

Other materials are used for containers, particularly fibreglass and metal and, provided their shape is suitable, and the colours are restrained, they will be perfectly satisfactory. The only drawback is that fibreglass containers have a high casualty rate as they can be quite fragile. Hostas will grow quite happily even in conventional metal wire hanging baskets although, in these, they are not entirely safe from slugs and snails, which have been known to climb walls to get to tasty hanging baskets!

The ultimate containers are stone – very expensive and virtually indestructible. Reconstituted stone containers are available and these are also very suitable for Hostas. Good troughs can be found in these materials and are very suitable for the very small Hostas. There is no limit to the use of recycled materials for plant containers – these are all right if you wish to be seen as eco-friendly or

for novelty value, but conventional containers are much better for the serious Hosta grower.

The success for growing Hostas in containers is very much controlled by the size of the container selected for your plants. It is always assumed that if a young Hosta is planted in a large pot and fed like mad, it will rapidly grow into a large plant. This is very far from the truth and a surprising number of Hostas have been lost through being planted in too large a pot with too large a volume of sterile compost. This does not apply to plants growing in the garden soil, because this is a living entity, and the plants in the garden share the soil with some weeds and many other living organisms that keep the soil fresh. For the small Hosta in a large pot, it is possible that moisture is drawn away from the plant in the centre, or that the unused compost becomes stale and stagnant due to the lack of biological activity in it.

It is very important that the size of the Hosta is balanced with the size of container in which it will grow. A Hosta purchased in a pot having a volume of about a litre should not be planted into a container greater in diameter than 8in (20cm), and possibly a smaller container if it is a small Hosta variety. This is not cruelty to the Hosta – they will establish better and grow a good root system

This display of potted Hostas shows that a modest size pot will accommodate surprisingly large Hostas.

very much faster in a suitably sized container. Our experience with growing hundreds of thousands of containerized Hostas over more than twenty-five seasons has proved this time and time again.

COMPOSTS FOR CONTAINERS

The right choice of compost is as important as the choice of container and it is unreasonable to expect a Hosta to grow well in cheap, unimproved compost. Our experience with growing these plants in pots shows that it is essential to use good proprietary composts which are specifically recommended for growing on plants in tubs, baskets, and containers.

Multipurpose composts are only really suitable for raising seeds and cuttings, and growing very young plants, and such composts generally only contain sufficient nutrients to last the plants for a few weeks. The composts recommended for tubs, baskets and containers are generally coarser and provide a greater volume in the compost for air and water, and enable better drainage of surplus water. They also contain a much higher quantity of plant nutrients.

Many people are tempted to use garden soil in containers but this soil will contain many weed seeds and much other plant and animal life, some of which will be undesirable for the health of your Hosta, such as vine weevil larvae (grubs), slugs and snails and their eggs. These weed seeds and pests will have been removed during sterilisation of the proprietary composts. Some growers are also tempted to use mixtures of different types of composts but this is unwise as such mixtures can be both variable and untested. With composts you really do get what you pay for and the well-known compost manufacturers will have carried out extensive trials to ensure that their compost is suitable for the purpose for which it is recommended. Our nursery pays a wholesale price for compost which is higher than the retail price for multi-purpose composts at garden centres, and we consider that this money is very well spent.

There are enormous differences of opinion as to what type of compost is best suited for growing Hostas and other plants in containers. The large scale raising of plants in containers is relatively recent, although the Victorians grew plants in containers, but to a much lesser extent. It is not so long ago that nurseries used to dig up plants in the autumn and spring, wrap them in newspaper or hessian and supply them to customers in this way. As container-growing for sale

Examples of proprietary composts that are suitable for growing Hostas in containers.

of plants all year became more widespread, the growing media or compost has been the subject of increased research. The well-known John Innes composts became the most commonly used in the 1930s, and these were mixtures of loam from composted grass turves, peat, sand and added nutrients. These, despite containing significant amounts of peat, are described as soil or loam based composts.

In the 1970s lighter soil-less composts based on peat were developed. In addition to the relatively inert peat, these composts included lime to neutralize the acidity of the peat, nutrients and sometimes sand, grit or vermiculite for specified purposes for the composts. At that time plentiful supplies of good quality peat were available from Northern England, Somerset and Ireland, but it now comes from many other countries. Peat is produced by the degradation and rotting either of sphagnum moss for the better quality peats, or by the degradation and rotting of grasses and sedges for the coarser peats. Generally, the extraction of peat from the ground is now subject to controls and Codes of Practice as peat is a material which is slow to regenerate and must no longer be taken from Sites of Special Scientific Interest. The current annual peat extraction on an international scale is now less than the rate of natural peat production, but it is still sad to think that the majority is used for fuelling power stations. The UK Government is committed to a reduction in the usage of peat and alternative materials are being evaluated for use in peat-free composts. These materials include composted bark and other forestry by-products, green waste, coir and others. For general mulching and soil conditioning suitable alternatives to peat are available, but for potting composts, it is at present proving difficult to provide alternative materials that are as effective and reliable as peat. There are undoubtedly some good quality peat-free composts for growing plants that need no special management.

There are advantages and disadvantages to the use of loam-based as opposed to peat or organic-based soil-less composts. Soil-less compost is lighter, easier and more pleasant to handle. They hold a great deal more water but dry out more quickly and are harder to re-wet. However, they are well-aerated and less prone to water logging. Loam-based composts due to their greater weight give more stable containers for exposed or vulnerable situations in the garden. They are also perhaps preferable for the more long-term containers. Hostas, however, do respond well to more frequent re-potting. Our nursery has always used soil-less composts and favours these over the loam-based composts. This is mainly due to their lightness and ease of handling when potting large numbers of containerized plants. For the gardener the loam-based composts will also give good results and are recommended by many gardening experts.

There are several grades of John Innes composts.

Hosta 'June', an outstanding variety which performs extremely well in a container.

First there is John Innes seed compost, containing nutrients for early development only and which are for growing seeds and rooting soft cuttings. John Innes Compost Number 1 is for potting young seedlings or rooted cuttings and John Innes Composts Numbers 2 and 3 are for general potting-on of plants. The Number 3 contains more nutrients and is suitable for vegetables, mature plants and shrubs. There is also a John Innes Ericaceous Compost which is lime-free and is formulated for acid-loving plants. John Innes Number 2 is best for potting Hostas as too much nutrient can lead to scorching of the Hosta plant's foliage, and using this compost gives the flexibility of being able to add more nutrients at the time of potting or later.

There is a selection of soil-less composts and these can vary from fine to coarse grades and from low to high in nutrients. Where there is a choice, Hostas are best suited to medium grade and medium nutrient content. Container, tub and basket composts available from garden centres are likely to fall into this category. Some will contain added loam and these are equally suitable.

CHOICE OF HOSTAS FOR CONTAINERS

With medium to very large Hosta varieties it is always best to plant a single Hosta in a round container and allow it to grow to maturity, re-potting it when necessary. A slightly quicker

Different Hosta varieties growing together in the same container seldom give a satisfactory display.

result can be achieved by having three or more plants of the same variety together in the pot, but three one-year-old plants will never look as good as one three-year-old plant. There is also the temptation to have more than one Hosta variety in the same round container but this seldom gives a satisfactory result except with the small and very small varieties. With oblong containers,

Hostas can grow harmoniously with a range of companion plants in containers, but do not let the Hostas get swamped.

ABOVE: *Hosta* 'Fire and Ice' and the smaller *Hosta* 'Fireworks'. The foliage is shown off against a similar colour container.

BELOW: Small Hostas in fibreglass troughs in a display at the Chelsea Show.

it will obviously be necessary to have more than one plant but in this instance two of the same variety achieve a better effect. Medium to large varieties grown too close together in the same pot means that neither of them is able to grow into a good uniform plant and this results in a rather muddled arrangement which does not show either variety at its best.

If a mixture of a Hosta with other plants is required, particularly where the pot is too large for the Hosta alone, this can be done and the companion plants can be removed as the Hosta grows to fill the pot on its own. Care must be taken to ensure that the Hosta does not get swamped by other plants growing in the same container.

A small variety can look good with just one to the pot but mixtures of the small and very small Hostas do grow very well in troughs and similar containers. All Hosta plants like to get their roots down to the bottom of their containers and therefore these should be shallower for the smaller varieties.

The final choice of which varieties to grow in containers is a matter of personal preference. It is very difficult to select any variety as being less suitable for growing in a container. After growing hundreds of Hosta varieties in thousands of pots annually for more than twenty-five years, it has been impossible to name any popular variety that has been consistently and significantly inferior.

PLANTING THE CONTAINERS

Good water drainage is essential for containerized Hostas. If a container does not have one or more good drainage holes in the base, then some should be drilled. When the planted container is placed on the ground it is important that these drainage holes are not obstructed and the use of feet to raise the pot is a good idea. The base of the container should now be filled with drainage material to a depth of 1–2in (25–50mm). Suitable materials are broken clay pot pieces (crocks), coarse gravel, polystyrene chippings or any suitable coarse, inert, non-degradable material that will allow the passage of water.

The best results are achieved by the addition of further ingredients to the potting compost. First, should the compost not contain horticultural grit, this should be added at a rate of just less than 10 per cent (6 litres of grit to a 75–80 litre bag of compost). The grit assists with good drainage and adds a bit more weight to the pot. Secondly, the addition of proprietary controlled or slow-release fertilizer granules, such as Osmocote or Phostrogen slow release plant foods at half the recommended rate is strongly recommended. Too much nutrient in the compost will make the Hosta more liable to the risk of scorched leaf edges. The controlled-release plant food granules should supply all the additional nutrients the Hosta will require for the full growing season.

A water-retaining gel can be added to the compost, but unless the containers are likely to be left without water for excessively long intervals, the

Interesting botanically, but mosses and liverworts can be a serious nuisance weed in container grown Hostas.

addition of the water-retaining gels are not necessary for Hostas. Commercial growers often add a low dose of a granular systemic insecticide to the compost. This gives control of vine weevil grubs, together with sap sucking insects such as aphids. More information is given in Chapter 7.

The added materials need to be well mixed with the compost to ensure even distribution. Place a one-inch layer (25mm) over the drainage material in the base of the container. The Hosta now needs to be prepared for planting; if it is a bare root plant these roots need to be spread out, and if it is a potted plant, remove it from its container and tease out the roots at the sides and base of the root ball. In either case cut off any obviously rotted and blackened roots, but otherwise they are best left untrimmed. Hold the Hosta in the position it will occupy in the container. If it is a dormant plant hold it so that the tip of the bud is about one inch (25mm) below the top of the container. If it is a growing plant hold it so that the position of the soil

level on the plant is about one inch (25mm) below the level of the top of the container. Even when the plant has bare roots, it should be possible to see (or guess) the correct depth that the Hosta should be planted in the new container. Whilst holding the Hosta in position fill the area below and around the Hosta with potting compost, gently firming it as you go until reaching about one inch below the top of the container. The gap is essential so that when the plant is watered the water does not run off the top of the container taking the compost with it. After watering, the level of the compost may drop in the container, so more should be added to bring it up to the correct level.

A topping of about half an inch (12mm) of chipped bark, grit or gravel, or other inert mulch will improve the appearance of the planted container, and will also suppress the germination of any weed seeds, and the growth of mosses and liverworts which can look very unsightly on containerized plants.

WATERING AND FEEDING

Once planted in the container, the Hosta must be well watered, completely filling the top of the container with water. Thereafter, the containers need to be regularly watered sufficiently to keep the compost moist rather than wet. Hosta containers should not be placed in a dish of water as the compost can become saturated. This may be done for intervals of up to two weeks or so if for any reason the plants cannot be watered normally during this time. The frequency of watering depends on climatic conditions and how much water the container can hold. In hot, dry and windy weather the Hostas will require more, perhaps daily watering. Large Hostas in smaller pots will also need to be watered more frequently. The ideal is to instal a simple water drip irrigation system. Inexpensive kits are available which are designed for containers, including hanging baskets and window boxes, which are harder to reach with a watering can.

On the subject of feeding, opinions differ very widely, and recommendations can be given from weekly feeding to virtually nothing except for what is in the compost at planting. Our recommendations are based on many years' experimentation and experience of raising a very large number of specimen plants in large pots and sales plants in smaller pots. Overfeeding of Hostas, whether in the ground or in containers, is not good as it will lead to the production of weak floppy growth which is susceptible to adverse weather conditions and furthermore makes the plants more attractive to predators. For this reason we advocate minimum feeding to maintain a healthy plant with sturdy leaf and flower stems and firm foliage.

As with Hostas growing in the garden, those growing in containers need the main elements, nitrogen, phosphorus and potassium, for growth, together with smaller quantities of magnesium for chlorophyll, calcium for cell walls and sturdy stems, and sulphur for protein production and enzyme activation. Other elements are required by plants in trace amounts only, such as boron, which is involved in cell division and production of amino acids, the building blocks for proteins and DNA, chlorine and copper for photosynthesis, manganese and molybdenum for nitrogen metabolism and zinc for carbohydrate metabolism. Plants are surprisingly complex organisms and deficiency in any of these elements can result in poor plant growth and undesirable symptoms, where it is not always easy to diagnose which element is deficient. The use of the correct fertilizers and feeds will ensure that there is no occurrence of these symptoms.

The controlled- or slow-release plant food granules will provide all the necessary elements in the required concentrations for growth of the plants from its earliest stages. These elements for growth will be depleted as they are used by the plants and also as they are washed out of the soil (leached) as soluble materials. The great advantage of controlled-release feeds is that the elements are released into the compost as they are needed and there will normally be no necessity for topping these up during the season.

Where a controlled release feed has not been incorporated into the compost at planting they can still be applied as a dressing to the surface of the compost in the early spring before Hosta emergence as nutrients will only be released when the weather starts to warm up. Alternative materials can also be applied at a later stage particularly if the containerized Hosta has not been re-potted for some time and the compost has become impoverished. The use of fertilizers recommended for fruit, vegetables, shrubs or bedding plants are not appropriate for hardy perennials, including Hostas in containers as they will contain high levels of nitrogen, phosphorus and potassium and will often include little or none of the other elements required by the plants. The use of all-purpose plant foods is essential for Hostas and many other plants. Many products are available but it is always best to use those from well-known manufacturers, and these include Phostrogen, Miracle-gro, and organic liquid seaweeds. These products also contain all the elements required for good plant growth, without any being available in excessive concentrations. Usually just two applications are necessary, the first when the plant starts into active growth and the second in mid-season, late June to July.

OVERWINTERING OF HOSTAS IN CONTAINERS

On balance it is best to over-winter Hostas under cover though many people will leave them out and the Hostas will grow perfectly happily the following spring. If it is not possible to move the containers, a waterproof cover, or even a sheet of polythene, can be placed and secured over the container. Wherever the container is placed the Hosta still needs its cold dormancy with plenty of frosty nights. Suitable places include carports, garden sheds, cold frames, and unheated garages and greenhouses. Sub-zero temperatures can cause the composts in containers to dry out and these need to be inspected every few weeks to ensure that the compost is still moist, and should if necessary be watered. It is not just the low winter temperatures which can cause problems, but the combination of waterlogged compost and hard frosts which can damage both plant and container. Over-wintering under cover will mean that the compost in the container will be nowhere near as wet as when left in the open.

Should a saturated pot be subjected to a period of extremely cold weather, frost will penetrate the container from above unless there is snow cover, but more importantly will penetrate the sides of the container. In very wet and frozen compost this can damage the Hosta root system and leave it vulnerable to fungal and bacterial decay. It is unlikely to kill the Hosta but can very definitely leave a much-debilitated plant for the following spring.

REPOTTING OF HOSTAS IN CONTAINERS

Should containerized Hostas not grow well in the spring, they may have failed to produce a good root system in the previous season, or the plant may have been damaged over the winter. If this happens, the Hosta should be taken from the pot and any damaged or decaying roots should be cut off cleanly. The Hosta should then be re-potted in

Some suitable plant foods for Hostas in containers.

Once the shoots of the potted Hostas appear close to the side of the pot, the plant needs to go into a larger container.

the smallest size container that will comfortably accommodate its root system. The temptation to give it any extra feed or tonic should be avoided since to apply this to an already stressed Hosta can only lead to further damage. A fresh potting compost mix will be very much better for the Hosta.

We have found that the best containerized Hostas are those which are re-potted every year, preferably before the plant comes into active growth. The plant is lifted, spent compost teased away carefully from around the roots, particularly under the base of the root system, and then re-potted in fresh compost with a new ration of controlled-release nutrients in a container which allows an extra one to two inches (25–50mm) of space for compost around the existing root system.

Of course few but the very keenest gardeners are going to find annual re-potting necessary but the same re-potting procedure can be carried out every two to three years. To leave it longer than this can lead to reduced growth and poorer quality plants, but there are instances of Hostas being left undisturbed for seven years or even longer and still performing well. Hostas will happily tolerate quite cramped containers but once their shoots emerge close to the sides of their containers they do need to be re-potted.

The time will inevitably come when a Hosta can no longer be planted in a larger container and it will need to be reduced in size to be planted back into the same container or even a smaller one. This can be achieved by division of the Hosta and this will be described in Chapter 6.

RAISED BEDS

Small raised beds can be regarded as large containers, offering a more varied planting which can be changed seasonally or at chosen intervals. The size of such beds and the depth of the soil would determine whether the plants are treated as growing in containers or in the garden.

Small raised beds offer good planting opportunities for Hostas.

Other problems for Hostas in containers

Hostas grown in containers are still subject to the pests and diseases of those growing in the garden and these will be detailed in Chapter 7. Although Hostas are ideal plants for growing in containers there are a couple of other problems most often associated with growing Hostas in pots and tubs.

The picture below shows two pots of *Hosta* 'June'. When planted into their identical pots these two plants were the same age and size and both were growing in the same compost next to each other, but they have grown quite differently.

The pot on the right contains a Hosta that is looking very sick. Some varieties are more prone to this particular ailment than others. The most likely to be affected are *Hosta* 'June', *Hosta* 'Great Expectations', and *Hosta* 'Sum and Substance' and all of their related varieties. The cause of the plant's illness is uncertain but almost certainly physiological as no pest or disease is involved. When it occurs, fairly hard division of the affected plants including the removal of any woody rhizomatous tissue will

In rare instances, Hostas do not grow in containers exactly as we expect and hope them to do.

result in perfectly normal growth of the divisions in the following year.

The only other problem we have found, mainly with potted young plants, is where they produce a flower spike with some small leaves on it, but otherwise next to no foliage. This is believed to be due to the plant, in the previous year, entering dormancy, perhaps enforced by stress, when it was about to produce a flowering shoot. The following year, the plant had not forgotten where it had left off, and instead of producing foliage it grew a flowering spike. Do not cut this down as the green foliage and stems will still carry out photosynthesis. Providing the same criteria do not apply in the current year, it will grow perfectly normally the following year. Of the commonly grown varieties, the more likely to do this include *Hosta* 'Sum and Substance', *Hosta* 'Halcyon', *Hosta* 'Patriot' and *Hosta* 'Whirlwind', but there are others that will also do this.

Young plants occasionally send up flower shoots instead of foliage. Next year's growth should be normal.

CHAPTER 6

Propagation of Hostas and raising new varieties

Each method of propagation determines the ways in which new Hostas can be raised. Division of Hostas is the usual propagation method which provides new plants identical to the parents. On rare occasions Hosta plants can produce some growth that is different in appearance and is termed a sport. Division is the method by which these sports are separated from the parent plant, possibly eventually to be a new variety.

For the commercial grower, division of growing plants is a very slow method of producing plants for sale and there is another method of vegetative or asexual (without fertilization in the flowers) propagation available. This enables very large quantities of plants to be produced in a relatively short period of time and is termed micropropagation or tissue culture. During this procedure it is likely that plants can arise which are different from the parent plant. Again, this can lead to the development and introduction of new varieties.

In the wild Hostas reproduce through the formation, dispersal and the successful germination of seeds produced following fertilization in the Hosta flower. Because of the Hostas distribution in the wild, both ecologically and geographically, opportunities for cross-fertilization are infrequent. In cultivation it is a very different situation and open cross-pollination of Hosta varieties commonly occurs to produce different offspring. Controlled cross-pollination, or hybridization, is widely used by amateur and professional growers in order to produce new varieties.

Whichever method is used, the raising of varieties new to cultivation is a very slow process taking a few years, and very frequently considerably longer, from finding the new variety to its availability on the market. Bearing in mind that there are already thousands of Hosta varieties available to gardeners, development of new varieties can only be justified when these are significantly different from existing varieties. However, the temptation of raising and naming new varieties is a huge incentive for continuing the search and it is highly probable that there are still totally different and novel features yet to be discovered and developed.

DIVISION OF HOSTAS

Hostas can be propagated very easily by division of the crown (sometimes referred to as the basal plate), which is the rhizomatous tissue from which the shoots emerge above and the roots below.

In the last chapter, one of the great advantages described for Hostas in the garden is their long-term growth coupled with low maintenance. Hostas can be left for very long periods without the need for division. The Hosta plants take from three to five years to produce a good mature plant and, unless there is a very good reason, should not be transplanted or divided during this time. It is fair to say that if you divide your Hostas every couple of years you will never get good plants. Once the three to five years have elapsed the Hosta should have developed a crown, which can be divided into good-sized viable divisions. Quite naturally, the divisions will not produce such good growth in their first year after division as the original plant prior to division, and small individual divisions can sometimes revert to producing immature juvenile leaves for a season.

The fragrant flowers of *Hosta* 'Guacamole' with a visiting pollinating insect.

It has been suggested that the centre of the Hosta crown dies out with age. Certainly some varieties, notably from *Hosta plantaginea*, can leave an empty space in the centre of the clump but, for the majority of varieties, the new shoots remain in a tight circle which is as well filled in the centre as on the outside of the crown. It has also been suggested that division of a Hosta clump is necessary to freshen it up, but in our experience there is no evidence of this, provided the plant is adequately fed with nutrients to ensure healthy growth.

The most common reason given for division is to make the plant smaller and in the short term this is true, but the reduction in size may be accompanied by a reduction in quality of the plant. It is important that a large variety is allowed sufficient space to grow to its full size, and provided this is done division is not necessary. If only a smaller space is available a medium or small variety should be grown. Divided plants will soon regain their size, and in practice the clumps do not then increase in size at the same rate of expansion as in their earlier years.

Division is a useful tool when more plants of that variety are needed elsewhere in the garden, or you have been asked by a friend (and they need to be good ones!) for a piece of your prize Hosta. True enthusiasts have been known to refuse this request. In practically all cases the divisions, provided they are a reasonable size, will grow very quickly into new plants having exactly the same appearance and characteristics as the parent plant.

When to divide Hostas

Division of Hostas can be carried out at any time but if done when the plant is in full leaf, some damage cannot be avoided. There is no right time for division – on our nursery we start in September and continue all through the winter months until April. Our December and January divisions grow just as well as those made earlier or later. However, there are two good times for division, both of which allow this to be carried out in reasonable weather conditions. Which of the two is best depends entirely on which is the most convenient to the gardener.

The first and most frequently recommended time for division is early spring from when the Hosta buds can be clearly seen until the buds are no more than about 4in (10cm) high. At this time, although the soil will still be cold after the winter, the Hosta will have started active growth. This is a convenient time to divide because the extent of

Hosta 'Sum and Substance' at an ideal growth stage for division in spring.

Division at a later stage than this could result in some damage to the Hosta.

the crown can be clearly seen by the position of the buds and the decision made as to what size divisions are required. Once the crown has been divided individual pieces will need to be planted as soon as possible and kept well watered for several weeks until they are thoroughly established.

The alternative time for division is in early autumn from the beginning of September. Although the plant will still be in full leaf some damage to foliage can be accepted at that stage of the year as the plant will be preparing for dormancy. The soil will still be warm as it cools more slowly than the air, and should also be reasonably moist as the hot days of summer will be past. Divisions planted into this warm moist soil will settle quickly and although no further growth of the foliage is likely to be seen, there will be some root growth and healing of the cut crown surfaces before the winter. The divisions when first planted will need to be well watered, but only for a short while, as autumn rains will keep the soil moist. Some suggest cutting down all the Hosta foliage when dividing in the autumn but it is best to leave as much green tissue as possible and only to cut away that which is badly damaged. The enormous advantage of autumn division is that in the following year the divisions will grow away without the need of watering.

How to divide open ground Hostas

Before dividing a Hosta it is best, if possible, to lift the entire plant intact from the ground, preferably with a garden fork. This may be difficult with a large, well-established Hosta as it will have produced a dense mass of thick fleshy roots, and it may be necessary to divide it in place by using a sharp spade to cut the plant into about four equal portions. This will make it easier to lift the plant in four or more pieces from the ground. If just a single division is required this can be done while the plant is still in the ground, using a sharp spade to cut out a slice like a piece of cake. The gap left can be filled with fresh compost and the Hosta will very quickly grow back into it.

If it is necessary to use a spade, dig it into the ground between 6–9in (15–23cm) from the outside edge of the crown and cut the roots all around the plant; 6in for smaller plants and the greater distance for the larger varieties. It should then be possible to lever the plant out of the ground by inserting the spade at intervals around the plant and pulling backwards on the spade handle.

Once the plant is lifted, brush or shake off the loose soil from the top and sides or use a hose to wash off the soil to expose the crown at the centre

The crown of developing buds at the centre of a clump of *Hosta* 'Gold Standard'.

of the plant. If the Hosta is lifted in the autumn you will be able to see clearly where the stems are attached to the crown and if lifted in the spring the position of the buds is very obvious. The use of two garden forks back to back is sometimes recommended for dividing the plant. This is only suitable for a very few of the more fibrous-rooted Hosta varieties such as *Hosta undulata*. As a general rule this method causes excessive damage to the Hosta and is not recommended. Even

the use of a sharp spade can cause unnecessary damage as it may need more than a single stroke of the blade to cut through the crown, and very few people are able to apply the second stroke in exactly the same place as the first. The use of a sharp knife or a garden saw is much preferable. Using either of these tools it is possible to cut through the crown exactly where you want, leaving a neat straight cut, which will heal much more quickly than a jagged cut.

A neatly excised division removed from a Hosta crown.

A mature Hosta clump may be divided several times if you ensure that each division has buds and an adequate root system.

The great advantage of lifting the whole plant is that it can be placed on a bench so that it can be divided in greater comfort. You can judge the number of divisions that can be made, and this depends on the age or size of the plant. It is very definitely best to divide the plant into relatively few pieces with plenty of buds and roots so that these can be planted straightaway into the garden. Where more than a single division is required the plant can be halved, quartered or more, if possible cutting right across the centre of the plant, again into pieces like slices of a cake. If cutting the crown for multiple divisions the knife or saw can be carefully placed so that the fewest number of stems or buds are damaged. All a division needs is a single bud and some root, but such hard division is not normally recommended.

Once the Hosta plant has been lifted and divided, the space left in the ground can be freshened up by cultivation and the incorporation of plenty of organic material, and one of the divisions may be replanted in the same position. There is no problem in replanting with another Hosta as long as there is no chance that the previous plant was affected by virus disease. The other divisions should be planted or potted as soon as possible and watered well to prevent them drying out.

How to divide containerized Hostas

The method of division is very similar to that for open ground plants and is best carried out at the same times, though there is a bit more flexibility with Hostas in containers. The Hosta in its container can be placed on a bench or table at a comfortable height for working. The Hosta needs to be removed from the container, and if well-grown and ready for re-potting or division, it should come out in a single piece, probably with a mass of thick white roots, and little compost to be seen. This is not cruelty to the Hostas as they really do like to be tight in their pots.

Try teasing out some of the roots and removing some old compost from the root ball, particularly under the base and also over the top of the crown. If a part of the plant needs to be re-potted into the same container, the parent plant needs to be divided in such a way that the division for

A Hosta removed from a container showing a well developed root system.

A divided containerized Hosta showing a clean cut of the rhizomes.

re-potting is a suitable size for that container. The ideal is to cut the plant into three more-or-less equal portions, again like the slices of a cake, so that each division includes a portion from the centre of the crown. After the removal of some compost from the base one of these divisions will be ideal for going back into the same container. Quite a lot of roots will be cut by the saw or knife, but these will quickly re-grow. With sharp cuts to the roots, fungal infection is only rarely a problem, and dusting with a fungicide is an unnecessary expense.

Division is ideal for providing a modest number of new plants. On our nursery we have raised some new varieties where we start with just a single unique plant. Relying on conventional division alone, we would expect to have about twenty-five divisions after five years. Commercially this is too slow but there are ways to speed this up.

Two methods have been used which both rely on the presence of very small dormant buds on the crown which can be persuaded to develop more quickly so that a greater number of divisions can be taken. The first method is rather drastic but has been in use by the Japanese for very many years. At about the time that the flowering stems start to emerge from the crown the entire Hosta foliage is cut down to ground level. This stimulates the crown, without being removed from the soil, to develop the latent buds into active ones. With skilled knife-work many more divisions, each with an active bud, can be taken. These tiny divisions would need to be grown very carefully in pots for at least a season and possibly longer before they could be planted in the garden.

The second is the Ross method, which is useful for increasing the number of divisions where only a few young plants are available. Our nursery has used this procedure but only small divisions are produced which again will need to grow for a season in pots. However, all the divisions produced in this way have been true to the parent plant, which does not have to be cut down. Good, thick-growing shoots are selected and the soil moved to expose the base of each shoot. A knife blade is inserted vertically right through the centre of the shoot about an inch (25mm) above the crown. A cut is then made from that point down through the crown as far as the roots. An identical second cut is made at right angles to the first, so that the stem and crown is cut into four identical segments, each of which will subsequently develop active buds. Once the foliage has died off and the Hosta has become dormant the segments can be separated and grown on individually. This is a clever method which causes little or no damage to the parent plants.

Whilst Hostas cannot be grown from soft stem cuttings, it has been found that when a dormant Hosta crown is cut into slices about ½in (12mm) square and planted in compost, the majority of these pieces may grow latent buds to make new plants.

Hosta varieties that produce stolons are very easy to divide into many plants. Individual stolons with young plants already developing on them can be removed and grown on their own. Simple division of large plants however is still the preferred method for the propagation of stoloniferous varieties by the gardener.

COST OF HOSTA PLANTS

Hostas cannot be propagated true to their parent by the quicker and less expensive means of sowing seeds or taking cuttings. The usual methods of Hosta propagation are by division, which produces few offspring, and by micropropagation, which produces large numbers of offspring but at a very high cost. Plants produced by micropropagation, and sometimes by hard division, will need to be grown on for one or two seasons before they can be sold at a size suitable for planting in the garden.

Both division and micropropagation are expensive methods of propagation and there is sometimes concern at the apparently high cost of Hostas in relation to other hardy perennials. The cost is further compounded as over 90 per cent of the new varieties are raised in the United States. The cost of buying Hostas from American nurseries is high as the cost of shipping, and an official inspection for issue of a Phytosanitary Certificate, prior to export, together with the tax and duty payable on arrival in the United Kingdom, all have to be added to the total. Since all this can take up to three weeks and even more, there is an element of risk in the safe arrival of the plants.

Dutch growers are increasingly involved with wholesale and retail large-scale propagation of Hostas which is helping to reduce the enormous cost to Hosta specialists and general nurseries.

The prices charged by specialist Hosta nurseries are invariably based on the cost of the original stock purchased together with the relative ease or otherwise of propagation of the varieties. Invariably the newest varieties have to be the most expensive.

SPORTING OF HOSTAS

Sometimes Hosta plants can spontaneously produce a leaf or shoot which is different from the rest of the plant and this is termed a 'sport'.

Sometimes a variegated plant can produce some all-green foliage and while technically this could be termed a sport, it is more usually regarded as reversion as the plain leaves may well be identical to a parent of the variety. If plain leaves do appear in any of your Hostas, these should be removed as soon as possible. Should the problem persist the plant should be lifted and divided while the plant is in leaf, in order to remove the plain portion. Unfortunately, a few varieties, particularly the less stable ones, can be more prone to reversion.

Good sports are not common and our nursery estimates a distinct sport to occur once in about 40,000 plants though they can be much more frequent in newly micro-propagated plants. The problem is to remove the sport from its parent and to grow it on its own. Hostas are infinitely variable and some varieties like *Hosta* 'Gold Standard' are more likely to produce sports, but only those that appear significantly different from both the parent plant and also from all other cultivated varieties, should be developed further. The sport and the portion of crown to which it is attached need to be separated from the rest of the plant using a sharp knife to cut the crown. If this is successful pot up the sport and grow it on. Some suggest leaving a sport to grow for two or three seasons with the parent plant, but on balance earlier removal is advisable as the sport is usually less vigorous than its parent.

Once the sport is potted it should be grown on for the rest of the season. When it re-emerges the following spring there are several possibilities. It may have reverted to the parent plant, or prove to be too unstable, or is identical to a known variety, or just no longer interesting. It may still look good but need further division to separate it, or if you are very lucky, the division looks good and is totally free from parent plant material. Sometimes the sported plant may have shoots that look variable and continued division may be necessary to select the best result.

Streaked-leaved sports are very unstable and difficult to propagate. It is likely that no two streaked leaves on a plant are identical.

Once you have a mature sported Hosta potted up you can either keep it to yourself, or persuade

A single sported leaf in a clump of *Hosta* 'Aoki' (*fortunei*).

Sported white shoots in the golden leaves of *Hosta* 'Gold Standard'.

A frequently seen unstable sport of *Hosta* 'Francee'.

Hosta 'Frances Williams' sporting to the golden leaved *Hosta* 'Golden Sunburst'.

Considerable variation in divisions of a sport of *Hosta* 'Rippled Honey'.

Two different sports obtained from continued division and selection from *Hosta* 'Blue Angel'.

a specialist nursery that the new variety is good enough to be developed further. Bearing in mind how few Hostas become best sellers, the chances of success are not very good!

MICROPROPAGATION

For most cultivated Hosta varieties this is a very successful method of propagation, though streaked and less stable varieties cannot always be successfully and consistently propagated by this method. The keenest Hosta enthusiasts and collectors will always prefer divisions of original stock plants rather than micro-propagated plants. There will always be the suggestion that micro-propagated plants are in some way inferior to the original plant material, but good results are consistently achieved with this method.

Some stable varieties which regularly produce good micro-propagated offspring, very often give a mixture of two or even more distinct varieties, one of which is required variety. These and all micro-propagated young plants need to be checked to remove any which are not true to the variety being micro-propagated. Frequently, interesting variants are found and the process of micropropagation has itself given rise to many good new varieties.

Varieties that cannot be produced successfully by micropropagation will never become successful popular Hosta varieties, and we have to accept that the vast majority of the excellent and most popular commercially available Hostas are produced by micropropagation.

How micropropagation works

Micropropagation is capable of producing large numbers of plants by tissue culture, which can only be carried out under sterile laboratory conditions. There are those who have successfully micropropagated plants in the cupboard under the stairs in their home but this is exceptional and at the very least some expensive equipment is essential. This is very definitely a job for the professional micropropagation laboratories.

A low success rate in young micropropagated plants. All should have yellow centres.

A batch of micropropagated plants from a single variety showing a more or less equal mix of two variegated forms.

A very uniform batch of micropropagated *Hosta* 'Royal Golden Jubilee'.

Before considering micropropagation, plant material must be selected which is the very best available for the new variety and it is a serious decision to send the best of your scarce new variety to a micro-propagator. This material can be lost forever if the laboratory for some reason fails to produce any result, which can and does happen. Whatever material is sent it must be absolutely free of any fungal or viral disease since these can prevent successful micropropagation, or can be passed on to the micro-propagated offspring.

The principle of micropropagation is to take a tiny part of the plant, which may be stem or bud tips, flower parts, or other live plant tissue, and to surface sterilize these parts (now termed explants) in a suitable substance such as bleach or an organic solvent, followed by rinsing in sterilized water. In a sterile laminar airflow cabinet these explants are put onto a sterile, jelly-like growth medium containing plant nutrients and growth regulators in sealed, clear glass or plastic containers. The initiation of material for continued micropropagation can be difficult and requires very skilled handling as some explants can be grown on standard media whereas others require more individual and complicated media. These media must themselves be totally sterile to ensure no contamination by bacteria or fungi, which can grow very well on the media provided.

The containers for growth of the sterile explants have to be placed in suitable cabinets under very strict regimes of temperature, humidity, light intensity and day length. Once initiation into growth of the explants is successful, the next stage is multiplication of the plant material formed.

In multiplication the initiated material is physically divided into many pieces or treated with plant hormones to induce the production of many small offshoots that can be removed and re-cultured. Roots are not always produced during multiplication and under sterile conditions the offshoots or plantlets are treated with plant auxins to stimulate root initiation. Gradually the tiny plants produced can be hardened off and transferred from laboratory growing media to conventional potting media. They can then be gradually weaned to normal growing conditions for Hostas. These weaned plants are still very small and the one below is in a 3in (9cm) square pot.

Because of the huge number of hours of work required and the strictly defined conditions for initiation, multiplication and weaning,

Young Hosta plantlets growing in a nutrient jelly medium during micropropagation.

A recently weaned plant of *Hosta* 'Fran Godfrey' from micropropagation.

micropropagation is a very expensive process with no guarantee of success. Additionally the tiny weaned plants are going to have to be grown on perhaps for two seasons before plants are suitable for sale. It is possible to purchase tiny micro-propagated plants in small plugs of compost, but considerable skill is necessary to grow these and there are many disappointments. It is always very much better and more cost effective to buy plants ready for planting out in the garden.

HOSTAS FROM SEED PRODUCTION

As hardy perennial plants, Hostas produce flowers followed by seeds, which will produce new plants. A few varieties like *Hosta* 'Krossa Regal' produce sterile flowers which fail to set seed.

Probably only one species, *Hosta ventricosa*, produces seed that grows true to its parent. In the garden there are opportunities for cross-pollination in flowers by insects. Many Hostas can also be self-pollinated within the same plant and even within the same flower. Some natural hybridization can therefore occur and seed can be collected and

grown from these plants. However, it is extremely unlikely that plants grown from seed will look the same as their parent or even grow to the same size or habit. Many of our brightly-variegated plants are the result of years of selection and will never come true from their seed.

Seeds contain tiny embryonic plants with a supply of nutrients to enable seed germination and early growth of the seedling, all enclosed within a firm seed coat. The production of seeds by higher plants is a huge evolutionary achievement and has many advantages. It ensures the survival of the genus and also its spread through dispersal of the seeds. Seeds can remain dormant in the soil for several years if conditions for germination are not suitable and can therefore enable a genus to survive adverse conditions. Hostas vastly over produce seeds – successful germination in a suitable position is a matter of luck and many seeds will be lost. Natural selection of the seedlings also ensures only the survival of the fittest.

It can still be an interesting exercise to grow Hostas from seed, preferably in mixtures of seed harvested from many varieties to ensure some plant variation. Since Hostas freely cross-pollinate and hybridize they do not grow true to either parent.

The black winged seed of Hostas.

RIGHT: Seed pods forming after successful pollination of Hosta flowers.

However a wide range of plants can be grown cheaply and usually have plain blue, green or gold leaves in a range of shapes and sizes. Variegated seedlings can be produced from a limited number of variegated varieties.

Hosta seeds do not readily germinate in the soil in British gardens whereas, for example, in Holland where the water table in the soil is high and the surface is moist, the seed germinates in profusion and can become a nuisance! Where this is likely to occur, it is essential to remove flowering stems soon after the flower petals start to fall. The interval between fertilization of the flower and ripe seed being dispersed is six to eight weeks so there is some time for removal of fertile seed pods.

In cultivation a high percentage of seed germination can be expected. Seeds are best sown between November and mid-July, but if before March a propagator or bottom heat is necessary. Seed should be sown evenly in trays or individually in cell units in good proprietary seed compost and just covered with a thin layer of compost or vermiculite. The trays should be placed in a suitable, shaded position. If sown in the winter they need to be kept in a heated greenhouse or propagator. In spring and summer they should be kept in a

LEFT: Recently germinated Hosta seedlings in a range of shapes and colours.

bright situation under the greenhouse staging, in a cold frame or a safe position in the garden. It is important to keep the compost moist and not too wet. The seed germinates quite slowly, starting in not less that three weeks and continuing for several more weeks. The seedlings also develop very slowly and it is best to over-winter them in their cells or trays. When they are big enough to handle select only the more interesting plants and pot them individually in 3in (9cm) pots. Sometimes white seedlings are produced but none of ours have ever survived for long.

HYBRIDIZATION

Seed is the very obvious source of new Hosta varieties, but the seed breeding of these requires enormous patience, skill, knowledge and a certain flair, which with unlimited time can produce results.

Plant breeding involves the crossing of selected parents to produce seedlings which are selected either to be grown to produce a new variety at that stage, or to produce breeding material for further crosses.

To the novice, breeding is simply a matter of choosing a variety with a desired character and crossing it with a different variety of another desired character to obtain progeny with both the desired characters. This certainly does not always happen in practice though we can be encouraged by the achievements of the celebrated Eric Smith who crossed the large, blue leaved *Hosta sieboldiana* with the medium-sized thick green leaved *Hosta tardiflora* to produce a group of medium-sized thick blue leaved varieties.

Hybridizers are not necessarily looking for improved and new visible features but also for plants that are more garden-worthy with greater tolerance to wide-ranging and adverse conditions, and also increased pest resistance.

Many Hosta characteristics are carried on the genes which make up the chromosomes found in all the cell nuclei making up the plant. The inheritance of these characteristics follows Mendelian laws. Other important characteristics, particularly leaf variegation are non-nuclear and can only be transferred by the mother plant.

MENDEL'S LAWS OF INHERITANCE

Johann Gregor Mendel was an Austrian monk whose experimental work provides the basis of our knowledge of genetics. Between 1856 and 1863 he conducted trials with a total of about 29,000 pea plants.

He selected seven characters each with two variations in garden peas (*Pisum sativum*) such as green and yellow pods, round and wrinkled seeds, red and white flowers, and tall and dwarf plants. By crossing these peas and carefully counting and analysing the characters of the offspring he was able to make deductions, which later formed the basis of Mendel's laws. These concern the principles of passing of characters from parent to offspring through the inheritance of dominant or recessive genes following the cross-pollination of plants.

In Mendel's day the term gene was not yet in use but he recognized that 'factors' within the plant controlled inheritance.

In carrying out selected crosses it is necessary to decide on the pod or maternal parent, and the pollen or paternal parent. Before crossing the two, it is necessary to emasculate the flowers by removing the anthers that produce the pollen, to prevent self-pollination. At the time when the female is receptive, pollen is brushed onto the stigma with a fine camel hair brush or similar. This needs to be repeated several times to ensure that pollination takes place, all the time ensuring that the flower cannot be accessed by insects with pollen from another source. As the flowers fade, small seed pods are formed containing the results of your cross, which grow and when ripe will have turned brown and started to split open to release the seeds. Ensure that the seeds when harvested are placed in a brown paper bag labelled with details of the two parents, to fully ripen. These seeds, which sometimes benefit from stratification (that is exposure to sub-zero temperatures) can subsequently be sown and the seedlings grown on for evaluation.

Other techniques have been used such as exposing seeds or seedlings to chemicals, radiation, microwaves, and others to induce mutations but these are seldom successful.

DIPLOIDS AND TETRAPLOIDS

Hostas and most other plants are more usually diploids, which means that in every cell nucleus which makes up the plant, there are two sets of chromosomes, one from each parent. As plants grow their cells divide and each nucleus splits to give two nuclei with identical chromosomes, which will be present throughout the plant, including the male and female reproductive cells. These chromosomes carry the genes which determine the characteristics of every living plant and animal, and which are passed on by each parent in varying measure to their offspring.

A tetraploid has a double set of chromosomes and in the wild *Hosta ventricosa* is believed to be the only naturally occurring tetraploid species.

Tetraploidy, as well as occurring naturally in some plants or being inherited from their parents, can be induced by means of chemicals, particularly Colchicine. There is considerable interest in tetraploid Hostas and many such varieties are now available; these are often better in many ways than their diploid ancestors. Tetraploids have been shown generally to have thicker and stronger leaves and stems, improved colour, and better leaf variegation, though not necessarily all of these in every tetraploid. One other great advantage has been clearly demonstrated in some varieties, with white-centred green leaves, which have become very much more sun tolerant. A good example of this is the tetraploid *Hosta* 'Fire and Ice' which has been found in some situations to tolerate exposure to the sun for up to the whole day without exhibiting any scorching.

The figures on the following pages show four examples of diploids at the top, with one of its tetraploid progeny underneath.

In these examples the tetraploids are generally stronger and more attractive varieties.

Hosta 'Sagae'.

Hosta 'Liberty'.

Hosta 'Francee'.

Hosta 'Patriot'.

Hosta 'Golden Tiara'.

Hosta 'Grand Tiara'.

Hosta 'White Christmas'.

Hosta 'Night before Christmas'.

CHAPTER 7

Pexts, diseases and disorders of Hostas

Practically all plants, whether wild or cultivated, are susceptible to pests and diseases. The common oak *(Quercus robur)*, for example, has no less than seventy different recorded pests and diseases. While Hostas are affected by far fewer pests and diseases than many other cultivated and wild plants, they do include some of the most debilitating.

- **Slugs and snails.** As Hostas have a large expanse of foliage they are among the plants which can be most affected by slugs and snails, and these are quoted as being one of the most severe pests in the garden.
- **Vine weevils.** This is again one of the commonest and most serious pests affecting a wide range of cultivated plants in British gardens. Damage to the aerial parts of the plant is merely unsightly, but damage to the roots can be devastating.
- **Hosta virus diseases**. The importance of these should never be underestimated, particularly with the rather sudden spread of Hosta Virus X. Viruses are virtually impossible to control except by the total destruction of infected plants and by observing the most stringent precautions to prevent the spread of these diseases.

These are the major problems where control methods may always need to be in place. Hostas do have other pests; these are usually of local importance; or occur periodically; or are climate related; or are seldom or not yet a problem in Britain but may be common in other countries. These other pests include caterpillars (cutworms),

The red version of the Great Black Slug. This is one of the most voracious slugs and one of the most difficult to control.

birds and mammals, leaf nematodes, bacterial and fungal rots and physiological disorders.

SLUGS AND SNAILS

Britain's moist climate, without the extremes of high and low temperatures, does make it even more suitable for slugs and snails than the climate of most other countries, and as a result British gardeners do get blamed for taking insufficient trouble to control these pests. It is also not too surprising that Hostas have become synonymous with slugs and snails, and it is inevitable that many gardeners have been dissuaded from growing them because of the ravages of these pests. Undoubtedly Hostas, particularly young plants, are extremely susceptible to attack and can be devastated within a short period of time.

Damage by snails. Slugs eat the veins as well as the rest of the leaf.

Slugs and snails have probably been living on this planet for much longer than we have, and this does mean that we know a lot about them. We know their life history, their habits, their likes and dislikes, and this enables us to use the control methods which are going to be effective against them.

Slugs and snails are gastropods, which is derived from the Greek language and literally means 'stomach foot'. Within this family, slugs and snails are members of the huge group of molluscs, the vast majority of which live solely in water. Snails have very visible and sometimes ornate shells into which they can retreat to avoid their predators and to prevent desiccation. It is also very effective protection for their hibernation as they can seal themselves into their shells. In slugs, the shell has been reduced to a small internal horny plate, which makes them very much more susceptible to drying out when they are not in the damp shade.

There are fifty to sixty varieties of slugs and snails, a few of which are carnivores. Some feed on decaying animal and plant material, some happily graze fungi and the green algae which cover many objects in the garden, but many are found feeding on living plants, particularly those which we grow as vegetables and ornamental garden plants. Slugs and snails are born survivors and their success is undoubtedly due to their incredible adaptability to their environment. An example of this is their resistance to low temperatures. At one time gardeners could rely on a cold winter with plenty of night frosts to reduce their populations, but now slugs often hibernate in places with the very minimum of protection and have adapted to regularly surviving exposure to sub-zero temperatures.

They have a relatively short life span of two to six years, but are able to lay between 100 and 800 eggs every year between spring and autumn. To increase their chances they are hermaphrodites and do not necessarily have to mate to lay viable eggs, which are very characteristically pale or creamy gelatinous spheres about $\frac{1}{8}$in (3–4mm) diameter.

If these eggs are found during autumn and winter tidying of the garden they can easily be removed and then destroyed or left in the open

SLUG AND SNAIL CONTROL

Trying to control slugs and snails is very much like trying to lose weight. Both require a persistent, continuous, single-minded effort. With such dedication slug and snail populations can be reduced and good control achieved.

Some control methods require only a single decision and action, such as where to plant the Hosta (in a pot or whereabouts in the garden), which varieties to grow and which mulch to put all around the plant. All these and others are only partially effective as they are just deterrents and will only protect the Hostas in situations where slug and snail populations are low and where there are alternative food sources for them.

In practice only two control methods have shown consistently good results in actually getting rid of slugs and snails. These are the physical collection and removal of slugs and snails or the use of slug pellets to control them. Whichever treatment is used, it is absolutely necessary to start it before the end of February and to repeat it at frequent intervals.

A combination of different treatments is the ideal. Each method recommended gives some measure of control and the more methods that are used together the better. The level of control will be the sum of the controls achieved by each method.

Starting control methods after the damage is seen is too late. The start date quoted which is always remembered is St Valentine's Day on 14 February. If slugs and snails have been a problem in the past, they are going to be again, and treatment must be started by the time they are likely to be emerging after hibernation. Green tissue, even in the buds, eaten by these pests can never be replaced and therefore such damage must be prevented.

Even if good control is achieved in one season, some slugs and snails will have survived and these can quickly give rise to new generations. Total control is never possible and treatments will always need to be repeated each year to ensure that slugs and snails never get the chance to become a problem again.

Eggs of the Yellow Slug, slightly larger than life size.

The adults are able to eat double their body weight every day, and although their teeth are relatively simple and replaceable, they are reputed to have over 25,000 of them! They feed by a rasping action leaving ragged holes in leaves. The picture below shows where a Yellow Slug (*Limacus flavus*) has grazed the algae and other debris on the side of a polythene sheet showing the very characteristic pattern of their teeth. This large slug mainly lives on a diet of decaying vegetable matter but it can still damage growing Hostas.

Slugs and snails all evolved from ancestors who lived in the sea, still the home of many sea slugs, and the one weakness of terrestrial slugs and snails is that their survival depends on living in a moist environment. This requires that they are confined to shady and moist situations and that they feed actively from dusk and through the night when they are not exposed to warm, sunny or dry conditions. They are very much creatures of habit and every evening will follow their slime trails to the same feeding point. They do of course move very slowly but will travel up to about 25m each night. They also have a very strong homing instinct and will return quite long distances from where they might have been thrown!

for birds to consume. Slugs and snails will overwinter as eggs or as young or mature adults. Their reproductive rate is prodigious and fortunately many of the young do not live long enough to reproduce, but it still enables a very few slugs and snails to quickly re-infest any area where successful control measures have previously been in place.

The teethmarks of the Yellow Slug where the debris on the side of a polythene tunnel have been grazed.

The Yellow Slug, one of the largest slugs in Britain. Not usually found on live plants as it prefers to graze algae, fungi and decaying plant material.

Snails come in a wide array of colourful shells and sizes. The most usual is the garden snail (*Helix aspersa*), followed by various banded snails (*Cepaea hortensis* and *nemoralis*). Late in the season some very small, thin-shelled snails can be found on Hostas, and these can sometimes make small round holes in the leaves.

Of the thirty or so varieties of slugs, four are

Common garden snails in a group roosting on a tree trunk during daylight.

Banded snails in an attractive range of shell colours and designs.

The Large Black Slug with its newly laid clutch of eggs.

A Large Red Slug just emerging after recently being alarmed.

the commonest, and by far the most damaging to British garden plants. First is the Large Black Slug (*Arion ater*), sometimes known as the Large Red Slug and occasionally given the Latin name *Arion rufus*, but it can be either black or red, and also grey with virtually anything in between. It will grow up to 8in (20cm) fully stretched but when alarmed it curls up into a relatively small tight ball. In comparison with other slugs it is very thick skinned and when curled it is like a hard rubber ball and quite difficult to squash! This is a slug which can do a great deal of damage and is more

Small slugs similar to this can do a great amount of damage.

A small keeled slug, another of the most damaging garden slugs.

difficult to control, since being thicker skinned it can tolerate more open and adverse situations.

Three smaller slugs, ranging from nearly black through shades of grey and fawn, are, despite their size, extremely damaging to plants. These include the Field Slug (*Deroceras reticulatum*) at just under 2in (50mm) long, the Garden Slug (*Arion distinctus*) at just over 1in (30mm), and the slightly larger Keeled Slug (*Tandonia budapestensis* which, as the Latin name implies, has been brought in from Europe. They can be difficult to distinguish, but that is purely academic as all three need to be controlled.

Control measures are based on our knowledge that slugs and snails need a moist environment, are creatures of habit, and always go for the most accessible and palatable food. There are a number of control methods that can be used but any one of these on its own is unlikely to be sufficient unless populations are low. The best control will be achieved when more than one method described below is used simultaneously, and whatever measures are taken they should be in place before the end of February.

1. Growing Hostas in containers. This will make the plants less accessible to slugs and snails, but on its own is not enough to ensure that

A brand of copper tape. An effective slug and snail barrier on a container.

the Hosta will remain undamaged. Control can be slightly improved by raising the pots on feet, and placing copper bands around the pot, with fresh grease, Vaseline or WD40 around the top of the container. Other measures listed below for plants growing in the open ground may need to be taken as well.

2. Growing Hostas in damp shady parts of the garden is almost putting them into the slugs' and snails' mouths. It is much better to plant your Hostas in more open sunnier positions, and away from the places where slugs and snails can hide up during the day, such as walls, fences, stony and uneven ground, heaps of logs and garden rubbish. Regularly clear weeds, decaying vegetation and prunings as soon as convenient as slugs and snails will hide and lay their eggs under these.

3. It is well known that slugs and snails prefer soft, thinner leaved, easily accessible Hostas, in preference to those which have firmer, thicker leaves, and a taller, more upright habit. This is nothing to do with the colour of the foliage, though blue-leaved Hostas are often sturdier and thicker leaved than Hostas of other colours. For example the Hosta illustrated opposite has longer leaf stalks and a pronounced upright habit which make it much less accessible and palatable.

There are many other varieties which are less susceptible, but never completely resistant, to slug and snail damage and these include 'Abiqua Drinking Gourd', 'Barbara Ann', 'Beauty Substance', 'Big Daddy', 'Blue Angel', 'Blue Umbrellas', 'Blue Vision', 'Christmas Tree', 'Devon Green', 'Dream Weaver', 'Earth Angel', 'El Capitan', 'Fran Godfrey', 'Frances Williams', 'Gay Search', 'Gold Regal', 'Golden Meadow', 'Great Expectations', 'Green Sheen', 'Halcyon', 'Heat Wave', 'Iona', 'June', 'Krossa Regal', 'Liberty', 'Love Pat', *Hosta nigrescens*, 'Orange Marmalade', 'Paradise Joyce', 'Paul's Glory', 'Potomac Pride', 'Regal Splendor', 'Reversed', 'Sagae', *Hosta sieboldiana* variety *elegans*, 'Snowden', 'Spilt Milk', 'Sum and Substance', 'Thunderbolt', *Hosta tokudama* forms and varieties, 'Touch of Class', 'Whirlwind', and

Hosta 'Regal Splendor'. Tall leaf stems and thick leaves are a good deterrent against slugs and snails.

other varieties which would qualify to be included in this list.

It must be emphasized that these are not resistant varieties, and further control measures will be necessary in areas of high slug and snail populations.

4. Slugs and snails very much prefer not to have to climb over sharp barriers, or crawl over materials which are likely to be uncomfortable for them, though with their slime protection they can climb safely over razor blades! Materials used with a deterrent effect

A clear demonstration that soft leaved varieties are much more susceptible to attack by slugs and snails than larger thick leaved varieties.

Hosta 'June' growing in the open with a wide protective area of gravel which makes it much safer from slug and snail damage.

as mulches around Hostas include: gravel, grit, sharp sand, chipped wood, chipped bark, cocoa shells, nut shells, sea shells, sawdust, baked eggshells, pine needles, holly leaves, bran, hair, sheep's wool, coffee grounds, copper rings, and many more probably effective to a varying degree but too numerous to include. Acidic materials can also be effective and gardeners with more acid soils often have less trouble with slugs and snails.

The same slug species in different colours. They are not always deterred by rough surfaces.

It is very much better to use a mulching material that looks attractive as mulch and is readily available and inexpensive to obtain. No trial is likely to have been carried out to establish which is best so the choice is personal. One of the most popular materials is composted chipped bark, which has the advantages of looking good, being unlikely to be blown away by the wind, suppresses weeds, and is eco-friendly.

Plants may be used as barriers, and mint, chives, garlic, fennel, foxgloves and geraniums have been shown to have a deterrent effect. Kits of cables carrying an electrical current are also available, but when using these, one must be sure that there are no slugs and snails already within the area surrounded by these cables.

5. By a variety of means slugs and snails can be trapped and subsequently removed. The commonest method is beer traps, which visually give very satisfactory results. Several people have observed that it is a waste of beer, and one gentleman was heard to say that he did not believe in slugs dying happy! Beer is not always the best choice of attractant as slugs and snails have a well-developed sense of smell to enable them to find food. The use of beer may well bring in your neighbours' slugs and snails as well as your own and other more suitable attractants are sour milk or a weak Marmite solution. Other suggestions for traps include inverted grapefruit segments, damp carpet, wooden planks and paving slabs, which can be periodically lifted for slugs to be collected.

6. Physical collection of slugs and snails. Some laugh, others boast of their prowess of high scores of captured molluscs, but this does, unlike the deterrents so far listed, actually remove the slugs and snails from our gardens, and every one removed will be unable to produce further eggs and young. Collection of slugs and snails is best done at dusk or later, particularly when it is warm, and moist, as under these conditions they will emerge from the soil and other hiding places to search for food. Some people wear rubber gloves and

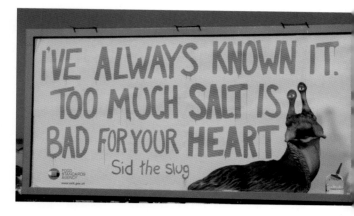

The slug and snail's aversion to common salt is well known.

collect them in a plastic bucket for later disposal, while others dispatch them in place by squashing, slicing, stabbing or pouring salt on them. The suggestion has even been made that mowing the lawn at midnight is a good control method.

7. Chemical control. This is not always the popular choice but it can be highly effective in controlling slugs and snails, and contrary to popular belief, correct recommended usage is very unlikely to harm wildlife such as birds, frogs and hedgehogs. Blue is a colour that birds do not associate with food and is therefore the colour generally used for slug pellets. A number of liquids have proved useful such as solutions of salt, magnesium salts, garlic, caffeine, and liquid metaldehyde formulations. The last could be regarded as preferable to pellets, and liquid metaldehyde is available as several different proprietary formulations and is particularly effective against the large black or red slugs, which on occasion do not respond to slug pellets. It is difficult to be certain but when watered onto the soil around Hostas there may be activity against both the eggs and the emerging slugs and snails.

Slug pellets must be very carefully applied and scattered thinly to give one slug pellet approximately every 4in (10cm) and never put in heaps or continuous rings around plants. Not only is it safer to apply them thinly, but it is more effective as a control measure.

The thin distribution of blue slug pellets needed around an emerging Hosta.

Slug pellets overall invariably give the best results and these are ready formulated for easy and convenient use. These pellets contain very small amounts of either ferric phosphate or metaldehyde, and should be applied shortly before or when the new Hosta shoots appear. The metaldehyde pellets will need to be reapplied at intervals of seven to ten days while conditions are suitable for slug and snail activity. The number of applications for ferric phosphate is more restricted but there is no limit to the number of applications of metaldehyde pellets as these break down quite quickly into carbon dioxide and water and do not leave any residues in plants or in the soil. It is highly specific for the control of slugs and snails, which only need to ingest a minute amount of active ingredient. Birds will not normally consume dead slugs but even if they did poisoned slugs are very unlikely to pose a risk to birds or hedgehogs. Additionally the metaldehyde pellets usually contain an animal repellent to prevent accidental ingestion of the active ingredient by wild or domestic animals.

As with all pesticides and weedkillers, it is imperative that the full instructions for safe and effective use are read and followed, as these are based on extensive trials and studies carried out with the products and their active ingredients to ensure that they are effective as recommended and that there are no adverse effects following their use. Particular care must be taken to store any unused product in the original container in a safe place, away from access by children, pets, and wildlife.

8. Biological control using nematodes. This method is suitable for the control of all common species of small to medium-sized slugs and also has an effect against some snails. The nematodes or eelworms (*Phasmarhabditis hermaphrodita*) for biological control are tiny wormlike creatures just visible to the naked eye and which seek out their prey, enter their bodies, killing them and finally releasing thousands more nematodes. The relationship between host and parasite is quite complex as the nematodes cannot exist for long without the slug host because they do not affect any other soil inhabiting organisms. It is therefore necessary to apply the preparation a maximum of three times at up to six-week intervals. The fresh nematode preparation must be drenched only on to moist cultivated soils at a temperature of 5°C or more. Most slugs will die below

The commonest predators of slugs and snails – thrushes, hedgehogs, frogs and newts.

the soil surface so the effectiveness of the treatment cannot always be appreciated.

It is always assumed that biological control is environmentally preferable but it is still important that the safety aspects of such methods are fully understood as biological and chemical control methods can both occasionally result in adverse effects.

9. Wildlife. The benefits of some species of wildlife in the garden can be very important for control of slugs and snails. While these are not necessarily their favourite diet, there are plenty of predators in the garden that will help to reduce the slug and snail populations. The most welcome of these are thrushes, which seem to be becoming more plentiful, hedgehogs, frogs and toads. Newts are always very helpful as they seem very partial to a diet that includes the eggs of slugs and snails.

Typical leaf notching by adult vine weevils on *Hosta* 'Hadspen Samphire'.

Other wildlife such as pheasants, partridges, certain ground beetles and some other insects, slow-worms, shrews and rats will sometimes feed on slugs and snails. The inclusion in the garden of wildlife areas including a small pool and other wildlife features will encourage these and other beneficial wildlife.

10. Domestic fowl. Ducks, chickens or bantams are for some gardeners the sole means of controlling slugs and snails. Our own experience has shown that chickens will peck and damage Hostas and other ornamental plants, but we have been assured that bantams, Khaki Campbell and Indian Runner ducks are excellent for slug and snail control with little plant damage.

In conclusion, slugs and snails can be controlled to varying degrees depending on the method chosen. Ten distinct methods have been described and undoubtedly there may be many more which are effective but have not been covered here. It is important that as many different methods as possible are utilized as it is the combination of a selection of these that will give the best results. If it is necessary to use chemical treatments then the alternation of different active ingredients and

different formulations is again the most cost-effective treatment.

In evolutionary terms it has to be said that slugs and snails do have their uses as they assist in the natural breakdown of decaying materials. So far as living plant material is concerned there is a limit to how much they consume and while they can reduce a young Hosta plant to ribbons this is never likely to be fatal for established clumps. Indeed it is another reason for growing Hostas to maturity as they then produce such enormous quantities of leaves that the damage is progressively less in such clumps.

VINE WEEVILS (*OTIORHYNCHUS SULCATUS*)

Infestations of vine weevil can cause great damage to many perennial plants. Hostas are not generally too badly affected except when they are growing long term in containers, particularly when peat-based composts are used.

There are three stages in their life cycle. The slow-moving adults normally feed at night and if disturbed play dead and fall motionless to the ground, so can be caught and removed when seen in the evening. These adults will cause notching of the leaf edges of plants but in Hostas this is restricted to relatively few varieties. In our nursery *Hosta* 'Hadspen Samphire' is usually the worst affected.

The adult vine weevils lay their eggs on the soil surface close to suitable host plants, and just to cause confusion these are not necessarily the ones they fed on as adults. Eggs hatch within two weeks and the creamy white and pale brown headed larvae (grubs) burrow down into the soil and feed on the roots of the plants, and in doing so reach about ½in (12mm) long. The greatest damage is done in the summer, but feeding continues until December, when they pupate to remain dormant during the winter, emerging as adults in the spring.

Knowledge of this life cycle enables us to plan suitable control measures, which can be cultural, chemical or biological. If containerized Hostas are re-potted every year in late autumn, any grubs can be physically removed and the life cycle broken. If the presence of vine weevil grubs is suspected lift the whole plant from the pot and remove as much compost as you possibly can from the rootball, or what is left of it. The grubs will come away with the compost and they make very welcome bird food. Re-pot the Hosta in fresh compost in a container that will comfortably accommodate the root system. Unfortunately several instances are known of Hostas being left in the same pot for several seasons and where the vine weevil grubs have then totally destroyed the root system and the rhizomes.

The grubs (larvae) of the vine weevil. White C-shaped fat bodies with pale brown heads.

Placing grit or chipped bark around the Hosta can discourage the vine weevils from laying their eggs in that pot.

Biological control involves drenching the soil around the plants in the open ground and in pots with a solution of the nematodes *Steinernema kraussei* which are sold as branded products. This needs to be done between March and November, though this timing can be limited as the soil temperature must be above 5°C at the time of application as the nematodes will not be active when it is colder. One application may be sufficient for a light infestation otherwise a second application may be necessary. Good control does require application in a high volume of water to ensure that the nematodes can reach the vine weevil grubs as they can only travel in the soil moisture.

Chemical control is very effective but still needs to be applied in a high volume of water. Our nursery routinely uses a very low dose of a slow release insecticide granule incorporated evenly into the potting compost as a preventative treatment against vine weevil larvae, as well as aphids and other nuisance flies. This and annual re-potting of all our Hostas ensures that vine weevil is never a problem. The same active ingredient with the common name imidacloprid is available to the amateur gardener as 'Provado' for use on all ornamental plants in pots and containers. A maximum of three applications is currently permitted from spring onwards, but will give control of vine weevil larvae for up to four months with light infestations.

VIRUSES IN HOSTAS

It is extremely worrying that viruses, which have been a relatively minor threat in the past, have now become a more serious problem. Viruses are naturally present in plants in the wild and inevitably growing varieties of such plants widely in our gardens will increase the spread of pests and diseases in general. The big problem with viruses is that there is no known cure and they can only be kept under control by using strict vigilance and ensuring total destruction of all infected plants to prevent their spread onto healthy plants. Cutting of plants to remove infected portions is not enough

as the whole plant will be infected even if other parts are not showing symptoms.

Some six viruses are believed to be pathogenic to Hostas and by far the most problematic at present is Hosta Virus X (HVX) which was first reported in cultivated Hosta varieties in the United States in 1985. The usual symptoms of HVX are fairly distinct but there are others, and only an expert could identify whether these are caused by HVX or by another virus. There are of course many questions about HVX which are as yet unanswered and research has fortunately been initiated in the United States to obtain more information on the behaviour of the Viruses to enable us to understand them better and to formulate more effective control methods.

The picture shows several varieties of Hosta affected by a range of symptoms attributed to virus disease.

The distortions and streaks illustrated are very definitely not typical of the varieties concerned, but these are the kind of effects that would be associated with viral infections. Symptoms include yellow, orange or green streaking, mottling or speckling, darker veins and 'ink bleeding', leaf necrosis, together with distortion of individual leaves or the whole plant. Streaking and mottling can be features of some Hosta varieties and should not then be mistaken for virus, though such varieties must always be suspect for virus infection. Hosta varieties found to be the most susceptible to HVX are 'Gold Standard', 'Striptease', and 'Sum and Substance', and many others are susceptible to a lesser degree. Very few Hosta varieties have been reported to be resistant or immune. HVX is present and is transported in the sap of infected Hosta plants. It appears unable to persist for long in the soil, but should you have to remove an infected plant, it would be wise to allow an interval of several weeks before planting another Hosta in the same place. Any action that involves cutting of the plant with any type of tool can spread the virus to another Hosta if the same tool is used on it. The greatest risk is in the division of

Various symptoms indicative of virus diseases. Top left is *Hosta* 'Striptease' and top right is *Hosta* 'Sum and Substance' both infected with Hosta Virus X.

Hostas and in cutting off any plant parts such as damaged leaves and flower stems. It is essential that the tools used are sterilized in organic solvents, household bleach or anti viral-disinfectants at frequent intervals, preferably after the cutting of each plant. HVX is specific to Hostas and plants can take several years to exhibit the symptoms, so the removal and destruction of just the plants exhibiting HVX symptoms is no guarantee that other plants adjacent are not infected.

Virus diseases are also in many instances transmitted by sap-sucking insects such as aphids, and it is a wise precaution to keep these under control. Fortunately neither Hosta seed nor pollen from Hosta flowers are likely to pass on HVX.

OTHER PESTS OF HOSTAS

Some further pests and diseases may be localized at present but the movement of Hostas between continents and between countries can, despite the inspection of plants at their point of entry into each country, still lead to the spread of pests and diseases. One example of a disease restricted to a country is the problem of leaf nematodes in Hostas in the United States. This is a not a problem yet encountered at our nursery in Britain, but there are of course other perennials, particularly *Anemone x hybrida*, that can be infested with related leaf nematodes. Nurseries and commercial growers should keep a careful check for any outbreaks in Hostas; the symptoms are a fairly characteristic dead streak between leaf veins.

Caterpillars (Cutworms)

On rare occasions holes in leaves may be made by the caterpillars of moths and sawflies. Feeding is more usually at night, and pictured overleaf are two caterpillars caught in the act – these are the only times that we have ever seen caterpillars feeding on Hostas. If in doubt, slugs and snails will always leave evidence of slime trails, which caterpillars do not.

If you find caterpillars, simply remove them, but do not handle the hairy ones with bare hands as they can sometimes cause a painful rash.

Hosta leaves being eaten by moth caterpillars.

Sciarid Flies

These are also known as Fungus Gnats and can be a problem on ornamental plants, including Hostas, particularly under polythene or glass. Our nursery had a serious problem with these for several years but now we can keep them under control again with imidacloprid incorporated into the potting compost. This active ingredient is contained in 'Provado' and when used for vine weevil control will also prevent any sciarid fly infestation. Sciarids are small grey flies and their larvae are very small white grubs that live in the soil, feeding mainly on decaying plant material but also on growing roots. This causes localized rotting and possibly the transmission of virus disease. Certainly localized plant distortions can be found where sciarid flies are feeding.

Aphids

These are common sap-sucking pests of many wild and cultivated plants, and can sometimes be found on the flowers or young emerging foliage of Hostas. They are very small winged and wingless flies, which can be green, black or grey, depending on the species. They are particularly important as they are responsible for the spread of virus disease in many agricultural and horticultural crops including ornamental plants. They are unsightly, causing distorted leaves and general plant debility. Many insecticides and organic methods will keep aphids under control. Again 'Provado' used against vine weevil will also control aphids.

Mammals

In the United States, it is very apparent that voles are a serious problem, but in twenty-five years of intensive Hosta production, our nursery has only experienced one instance of damage by voles or mice. It was, however, a serious incident and I can fully appreciate the frustration of American growers who suffer this problem. It caused us significant loss in a large batch of *Hosta* 'June' potted in very coarse, straw-based compost. The roots and rhizomes of many plants were so badly eaten that the leaves and upper crown were totally detached and the rest of the plant was gone.

Rabbits can occasionally nibble the upper leaves of Hostas but seem to have a marked preference for other herbaceous plants, particularly for hardy geraniums, ornamental clovers and, best of all,

A Hosta which has been well grazed by a small deer.

purple-leaved plantains. Squirrels sometimes do a bit of digging around the roots of Hostas, either looking for their nuts, or getting some moisture from the Hosta roots, but are only a nuisance and not a problem. For those who have them, deer are a serious local problem. Deterrents do not appear to be particularly effective – as with rabbits, appropriate fencing is the best option.

Fungal diseases and disorders

It has not been possible on our Nursery to identify any pathogenic fungi or bacteria on Hostas. Many plants have very specific diseases such as rust disease on hollyhocks and mildew on Michaelmas daisies. Hostas do not have such specific diseases but can become infected with fungi when damage to the plant has occurred either above or below the ground. When, for example, Hosta roots in containers get severely frosted then fungal infection can be found at the site of root damage. Similarly, when Hostas, particularly the smaller varieties, are very wet at ground level, fungal rotting at the leaf bases can occur but only where these are stressed or dying. A third example is when Hosta flowers shed their petals which may stick to the upper leaves, then fungi can infect these dying petals and the area of the leaf which they cover. Similar rotting can occur when leaves get damaged by sun scorch, but it is only the dead or dying portion of the leaf which gets infected with saprophytic rather than pathogenic fungi. Hosta seedlings are as susceptible as any other seedlings to damping off caused by fungal disease, but this is usually because the seedlings may be too wet, rather than being attacked by a specific pathogenic disease.

As described elsewhere in this book, plant disorders can occur through lack of specific nutrients, and through injuries caused by climatic conditions, specifically frost, wind, and hail.

Two other disorders observed in Hostas include the 'drawstring' disorder and fasciation. The latter is a strange disorder for which the cause is not known and found not infrequently in vegetable asparagus plants. Occasionally the shoots, instead of producing the usual cylindrical shape, produce ones that are broad and flattened. These have no adverse affects on the plant, which will grow again normally the next year. Just once we have found this in Hostas.

The drawstring effect is a very apt description and several Hostas are afflicted with this ugly

A Hosta plant badly damaged by hail.

Hostas can be marked or damaged by debris falling from above. Here a Cupid's dart has penetrated a thick heart shaped leaf of *Hosta* 'Sum and Substance'.

The 'drawstring' effect in Hostas.

disorder. As the name implies it appears very much as though a thread has been sewn around the edge of Hosta leaves, and the two ends have been pulled to leave a cup-shaped and very distorted leaf. It affects a few of the white margined Hostas and is caused when the white leaf margin stops growth, whilst the centre of the leaf continues. This leads to subsequent distortion and the inevitable browning and tearing of the leaf margins.

To conclude, numerically, the problems associated with Hostas are few. It is just unfortunate that the few that do affect Hostas are such major ones, and include two of the worst problems facing British gardeners. Vine weevils are perhaps the least of these as well-proven control measures are available, and as with slugs and snails the alternation of treatments will always produce the best results. Slugs and snails can be controlled and hopefully the control measures suggested will be found effective, and it will be appreciated that several of the methods will never give anything but low levels of control. The gardeners who have a bad problem always assume that everyone else does as well, but many gardeners are able to grow Hostas without any more than simple deterrent measures. Viruses could become a yet bigger problem, but we will all strive to ensure that the risk is kept to very low levels. Unfortunately, with all pests and diseases, neither total eradication nor total resistance are ever realistic possibilities. New resistant plant strains can be produced but the pests and diseases will always be able to produce a new strain to break the resistance, and sometimes they can even be more virulent than their predecessors.

An unusual occurrence – a fasciated Hosta flower stem.

CHAPTER 8

Popular Hostas

With the very large number of Hosta varieties available, it is inevitable that only a relatively small proportion of these are in commercial production and available for sale to gardeners. There are several books available which illustrate and describe many Hosta varieties, and visitors to Flower and Garden Shows will also have the opportunity to see many of the newly introduced Hosta varieties, including the often scarce and unusual varieties.

Nothing is more frustrating than to see a really good Hosta variety only to find it is not available in your nearest garden centre and possibly cannot be located with ease anywhere else. The purpose of this chapter is to describe about one hundred varieties which are relatively easy to find and purchase, but which also have been in cultivation in gardens and nurseries long enough for us to know that they will do well in our gardens. It has been emphasized throughout this book that there are many differences between Hosta varieties apart from their appearance, and it is important that the variety you purchase will be suitable for the conditions in your garden.

The size achieved by individual varieties in the garden will depend on the age of the plant, the type and fertility of the soil, the climate and the amount of rainfall and other factors, so to give exact plant and leaf sizes can be misleading. For this reason varieties will be described as very large, large, medium, small and very small as defined in Chapter 3. Unless otherwise stated the recommended situation for the varieties is from shade to half the day in full sun, provided that the Hostas are planted in well-prepared soil and kept watered until they are established in their position in the garden.

Hosta 'Devon Green'

With the description of each variety is given the name of the person or persons if known who registered or introduced the variety, together with the country of origin, and the year of registration or introduction.

Hosta 'Abiqua Drinking Gourd'
(Walden West, USA, 1989)

This hybrid of *Hostas tokudama* and *sieboldiana* is a large variety with dark blue, very puckered, and pronounced cup-shaped leaves. The flowers are near white, sometimes with a very pale lilac tinge, in early to mid-summer. It is an extremely popular variety in the United States, but listed by relatively few nurseries in Britain.

Hosta 'Allegan Fog'
(Herrema, USA, 2000)

This hybrid of *Hosta fortunei* variety *albopicta* form *aurea* is a medium variety with very striking variegation. The glossy and wavy leaves have irregular dark green margins with green streaks and flecks over whitish leaf centres. It is a remarkably vigorous variety which quickly forms a dense clump. It has lavender flowers in mid-summer.

Hosta 'Aristocrat'
(Walters Gardens, USA, 1997)

This is a sport of the Tardiana group of blue-leaved *Hosta* 'Hadspen Blue'. It is medium variety, having blue leaves with creamy yellow margins, later becoming creamy white. It grows to form quite a wide low clump and has pale lavender flowers in late summer.

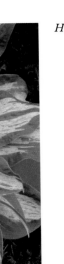

Hosta 'Allegan Fog'.

Hosta 'Aristocrat'.

Hosta 'August Moon' (Various, USA, 1997)

The parentage of this variety is not known, and although it was registered in 1997, it dates back to 1964 and is very widely available. It is large with broad golden yellow, moderately puckered leaves, which must have a sunny position to give a good colour. Pale lavender flowers appear in late summer. This is a relatively old, easy and popular Hosta, which is the parent of many popular modern Hosta varieties.

Hosta 'Barbara Ann'.

Hosta 'Baby Bunting' (Savory, USA, 1982)

This is a hybrid of an unnamed *Hosta* seedling and *Hosta* 'Rough Waters'. The variety is very small with tiny, round, grey blue leaves which darken later. It is a popular variety with very attractive purple flowers in early summer. Its variegated green-margined, yellow-leaved sport, *Hosta* 'Cherish', is particularly attractive, and an alternative to the popular but slightly unreliable *Hosta* 'Pandora's Box'.

Hosta 'Barbara Ann' (Muntons Microplants, UK, 1999)

This is a sport from tissue-culture *Hosta sieboldiana* variety *elegans*. Our nursery was involved in the early development of this large variety and was the first to list it in 2000. It is an impressive variety with greenish-blue leaves and cream margins. Unlike similar Hostas the drawstring effect has not been found in this variety. It produces near white flowers in early summer. For some unknown reason it was not proved as popular as might have been expected.

Hosta 'Beauty Substance' (van den Top, Holland, 2007)

This is a sport from tissue-culture *Hosta* 'Sum and Substance'. The large variety has huge, dark green leaves with yellow margins. In common with *Hosta* 'Sum and Substance' and its other sports it has thick waxy leaves which can tolerate full sun for much of the day, and if left to mature is likely to be able to reach a diameter of over 9ft (2.75m). It displays pale lavender flowers in late summer.

Hosta 'Big Daddy' (Aden, USA, 1978)

This is a sport of a variegated seedling of *Hosta sieboldiana* descent. It is a large variety with thick, round, heavy, dark blue-green puckered leaves and has white flowers in early summer. Our experience shows it performs best where it is only exposed to sun for less than a quarter of the day. It can also be prone to root damage by frost when left in an unprotected container over the winter. (This very popular, widely available Hosta is illustrated on page 8.)

Hosta 'Beauty Substance'.

Hosta 'Blue Angel' (Aden, USA, 1986)

This is a hybrid of two seedlings with characteristics of *Hostas montana* and *sieboldiana*. Very large variety with heart-shaped, slightly puckered blue-green leaves, and with a broadly spreading habit, which can reach a diameter of over 5ft (1.5m). It has near white flowers in mid-summer.

Hosta 'Blue Chip' (Benedict, USA, 1997)

This seedling from *Hosta* 'Dorset Blue' is a small variety with thick, intensely blue, round leaves. Pale lavender flowers appear in late summer. For its size and leaf colour it should be more popular than it is.

Hosta 'Blue Chip'.

Hosta 'Blue Mouse Ears' (Deckert, USA, 2000)

This is a sport of *Hosta* 'Blue Cadet' and is a very small and compact Hosta. The name is very apt because the leaves are thick, round, and slightly cupped. It has lavender flowers in early summer. The variety is a good grower and, very quickly and despite its newness, has deservedly become one of the most popular small varieties. Several very significant variegated sports have already been introduced.

Hosta 'Blue Umbrellas' (Aden, USA, 1978)

This is a hybrid of *Hostas tokudama* and *sieboldiana*. As its name suggests it is a large variety with big, dark blue-green, slightly puckered heart-shaped leaves. It is a very architectural plant which can grow into a clump over 6ft (1.8m) wide. Not as widely available as other large blue-leaved varieties.

Hosta 'Blue Mouse Ears'.

Hosta 'Blue Umbrellas'.

Hosta 'Brim Cup'.

Hosta 'Brim Cup' (Aden, USA, 1987)

This is a hybrid of *Hostas* 'Gold Regal' and 'Wide Brim'. It is a medium variety of brightly varie-gated, cupped, round and slightly puckered leaves. These are a rich green with broad pale yellow to white margins. Flowers are pale blue-lavender, lightening to nearly white, in early summer.

Hosta 'Buckshaw Blue' (Smith, UK, 1986)

This hybrid of *Hostas sieboldiana* and *tokudama* was developed by Eric Smith in the early 1970s. It is a medium variety with thick round, deep blue leaves which are heavily textured, slightly cupped and very puckered. It has near white flowers in early summer and looks at its best in a sheltered and shady position. Rather scarce but well worth growing.

Hosta 'Calypso' (Lachman, USA, 1987)

This is a hybrid of *Hosta* 'White Christmas'. It is a small, tight, clump-forming variety with lance-shaped yellow leaves which have broad dark green margins. It bears purple flowers in late summer.

Hosta 'Calypso'.

Hosta 'Carnival'.

Hosta 'Carnival' (Lachman, USA, 1986)

This is a hybrid from *Hosta* 'Beatrice'. The large plant has big, oval, green leaves with very irregular broad, bright yellow margins with streaks to the centre of the leaf. Lavender flowers appear in mid- to late summer.

Hosta Cat's Eye (Japan)

This variegated hybrid from *Hosta venusta* is a very small variety imported into the USA from Japan and available from 2001. It has tiny yellow but later creamy white leaves with dark green margins. Lavender flowers in mid-summer. This tiny Hosta has very quickly become popular and is ideal for growing in a shallow trough.

Hosta 'Cherry Berry' (Lachman, USA, 1991)

This is a second-generation hybrid of complex parentage. Medium variety with pointed, lance-shaped yellow leaves turning white with broad dark green margins. The great attraction of this variety is its purple flowers on their long bright red scapes in late summer. Probably it is best grown in a container as, having thin leaves, it is very susceptible to damage by slugs and snails.

Hosta 'Cherry Berry'.

Hosta 'Chinese Sunrise' (Various, USA, 1992)

This sport from *Hostas cathayana* or *lancifolia* is a medium variety dating back to 1960. Its attraction is that it is a very early variety having lance-shaped gold leaves, darkening later, with narrow green margins. Lavender flowers from late summer to early autumn.

Hosta 'Christmas Candy' (van Erven, Holland, 2002)

A sport of *Hosta* 'Night before Christmas'. It is a large variety with broad, lance-shaped, apple-green leaves with centres of creamy yellow, fading to white. Pale lavender flowers show in mid-summer, producing large white seed pods.

Hosta 'Chinese Sunrise'.

Hosta 'Christmas Candy'.

Hosta 'Christmas Tree' (Seaver and Vaughn, USA, 1982)

This is a hybrid from *Hostas* 'Frances Williams' and 'Beatrice'. The large variety has medium green leaves with yellowish white margins and there are near white flowers from early summer. This is a particularly robust and reliable variety and containerized plants can look perfect for the entire season.

Hosta 'Clifford's Forest Fire' (Clifford, USA, 2000)

A sport of *Hosta* 'Sagae' and a large variety with broad, blue-green leaves with very wide, irregular yellow leaf margins. Pale lavender flowers in late summer.

Hosta 'Christmas Tree'.

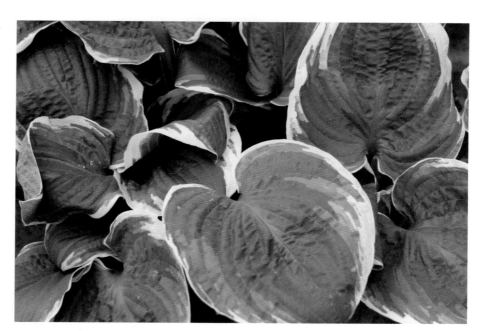

Hosta 'Clifford's Forest Fire'.

Hosta 'Cracker Crumbs'.

Hosta 'Cracker Crumbs' (Solberg, USA, 2002)

This sport of *Hosta* 'Shiny Penny' is a very small variety with tiny gold leaves which have dark green margins, making a very tight, compact clump. There are pale purple flowers in late summer. This is another very small variety that has quickly become extremely popular.

Hosta 'Daybreak' (Aden, USA, 1987)

This sport of a Japanese seedling is a large variety, not tall but spreading wide to a diameter of well over 4ft (1.2 metres). My opinion is that this is one of the best of all gold-leaved varieties. The leaves are broad, heavy, slightly wavy and puckered. Lavender flowers in late summer.

Hosta 'Daybreak'.

Hosta 'Diamond Tiara'.

Hosta 'Devon Green' (Bowden, UK, 2005)

This is a sport of *Hosta* 'Halcyon' and is a medium variety which forms a compact clump of thick, flat, dark green glossy leaves. It has lilac flowers in late summer. This variety was first available in the mid-1990's and not registered until 2005. Although it has plain green leaves, particularly impressive in a shaded position, it is a spectacular and very popular variety which beautifully complements just about any other medium or large Hosta. It is very widely available.

Hosta 'Diamond Tiara' (Zilis, USA, 1885)

A sport from tissue culture *Hosta* 'Golden Tiara', this small variety with heart-shaped green leaves has creamy white margins. It has purple flowers in late summer and is one of the very popular 'Tiara' series.

Hosta 'Diana Remembered' (Kulpa, USA, 1997)

This is a sport of *Hosta* 'Seventh Heaven' of *Hosta plantaginea* origin. Large variety with heart shaped, slightly glossy and wavy green leaves with yellow margins, later changing to white. It has fragrant white flowers in late summer to early autumn.

Hosta 'Dream Weaver' (Ruetenik & Walek, USA, 1996)

A sport of *Hosta* 'Great Expectations', this large variety with large, broad, dark blue-green leaves has a central splash of creamy yellow. It displays near white flowers in early summer and is similar to *Hosta* 'Thunderbolt'.

Hosta 'El Nino' (Warmerdam, Holland, 2004)

This is a hybrid of *Hosta* 'Halcyon' and a *Hosta tardiflora* selection and is a medium variety with smooth, heavy, textured blue leaves with yellow margins, later turning to white. Lilac flowers in late summer. Among the white edged 'Tardiana' Group of blue leaved Hostas, this is one of the best.

Hosta 'Dream Weaver'.

Hosta 'El Nino'.

Hosta 'Emerald Tiara' (Walter Gardens, USA, 1988)

A sport from tissue culture *Hosta* 'Golden Scepter'. Small variety with gold leaves with narrow green margins. The leaves are smooth, almost round, and slightly wavy. It has purple flowers in late summer and is one of the very popular 'Tiara' series.

Hosta 'Eric's Gold' (R. & M. Ford, UK, 2004)

A chance seedling of unknown parentage, this is a large variety with brilliant gold foliage, which makes a neat mound. Pale lavender flowers in early summer. One of the more impressive of all gold-leaved varieties.

Hosta 'Emerald Tiara'.

Hosta 'Fire and Ice' (Hansen, USA, 1999)

A sport of *Hosta* 'Patriot', this is a medium variety with dark green, well-textured leaves and broad, irregular creamy white leaf centres, turning pure white. This develops rather slowly as would be expected with a variety with so much white on the leaves. White foliage contains no chlorophyll and is unable to carry out photosynthesis. The usual moist and mild climate in the United Kingdom appears to favour the growth of this variety as eventually it will become a sturdy garden plant which, in a moist soil, can tolerate sun for most if not all of the day. Specimens in containers can be spectacular throughout the whole season

Hosta 'Fire Island' (Brinka, USA, 1998)

This is a hybrid of *Hostas longipes hypoglauca* and 'Crested Surf'. Medium variety with very striking wavy golden leaves which may turn greener later. The leaf stalks are deep maroon, and flecks of this colour reach up into the base of the leaves. It has lavender flowers in late summer and is an exciting introduction rapidly becoming very popular. It is relatively quick growing and another very suitable variety for the garden and for a container.

Hosta 'Fireworks' (Walters Gardens, USA, 2001)

This is a sport of *Hosta* 'Loyalist' which is very similar to 'Fire and Ice'. 'Fireworks' is a small variety with pointed, wavy edged and twisted white leaves with narrow, two-tone green margins and streaks to the leaf centres. It has light lavender flowers in late summer and is a vigorous and very dramatic variety which quickly makes a neat uniform clump.

Hosta 'Fireworks'.

Hosta fortunei variety *albopicta*

A natural sport of *Hosta fortunei*, this variety is believed to have been introduced in 1874, identified under the above name in 1954, and registered by the American Hosta Society in 1987. It is a most important variety and still grown and sold very widely. A large variety, which early in the season is very striking with green-margined, butter yellow centred leaves. Even if grown in a sunny position the yellow leaf centres will start to fade through shades of green, from early summer. Pale lavender flowers in mid-summer.

Hosta fortunei variety *aureamarginata*

A natural sport of *Hosta fortunei*, described in 1954, and registered by the American Hosta Society in 1987. This is still a very popular variety and is a reliable performer in the garden and in containers. It is a large variety with dark green leaves which have gold margins. It has to be admitted that there are more striking varieties with these leaf colour combinations but in the right situation it is still a very useful variety. It has pale mauve flowers in late summer.

Hosta 'Fragrant Bouquet' (Aden, USA, 1982)

This is a hybrid of *Hostas* 'Fascination' and 'Summer Fragrance'. It is a vigorous large variety and very popular, particularly as it has large, fragrant pale lavender flowers in early autumn. Large, heart-shaped, light green leaves with pale cream margins.

Hosta 'Fran Godfrey' (R. and M. Ford, UK, 2004)

This is a sport of *Hosta* 'Sum and Substance'. It is a very large variety with yellow-green leaves with dark green margins that can be very variable in width. It is a variety that will tolerate a very sunny situation when the leaf centres can be nearly gold. Pale lavender flowers in late summer. This has quickly become a very popular variety, and is now more widely available, including in Holland and the USA.

Hosta fortunei variety *aureamarginata*.

Hosta 'Fragrant Bouquet'.

Hosta 'Fran Godfrey'.

Hosta 'Francee' (Klopping, USA, 1986)

A sport of *Hosta fortunei*, and although registered by the American Hosta Society in 1986, was first introduced in the early 1970s. It was a quite remarkable introduction and for many years was one of the most commonly grown, white margined Hostas, and is still very widely grown and commercially available. It is a large and very vigorous variety making a neat clump. It performs well in gardens and is particularly effective in containers. The leaves are heart-shaped, smooth and dark green with narrow pure-white margins. Lavender flowers in mid-summer

Hosta 'Frances Williams' (Williams, USA)

A sport of *Hosta sieboldiana*, this was found in 1936 and registered by the American Hosta Society in 1987. This has always been an extremely popular and widely-grown variety. It is a very large variety having thick puckered, heart-shaped, blue-green leaves with a broad beige to gold margin. It has near white flowers in early summer.

Hosta 'Frances Williams'.

Hosta 'Gay Search' (R. and M. Ford, UK, 2004)

A sport of *Hosta* 'Krossa Regal'; like its parent, this is a very large, elegant, upright variety producing a vase-shaped mound. Named for the English gardening author and BBC television presenter of the same name, it has blue-green leaves with chartreuse yellow margins that slowly fade through subtle colours during the summer. It has lavender flowers in late summer.

Hosta 'Gay Search'.

Hosta 'Ginko Craig' (Found in Japan, registered by Craig and Summers, USA)

Probably a sport of *Hosta helonioides*; it was found on sale in Japan in 1968 and registered by the American Hosta Society in 1986. It is a small to medium variety quickly forming a tight clump. The leaves are quite long, slightly wavy and dark green with pure white margins and there are attractive purple flowers in late summer. With its low habit and thin leaves, it is very much at risk from slug and snail damage, and is safer growing in containers. If frequently divided it will remain in its juvenile form with very much narrower leaves and in this form is frequently used for edging borders.

Hosta 'Gold Haze' (Smith, UK)

This is a hybrid of the all gold form (*aurea*) of *Hosta fortunei* variety *albopicta* and *Hosta sieboldiana* and is an Eric Smith introduction which was registered by the American Hosta Society in 1988. Large variety with smooth, pale gold leaves which are superb when they first emerge in the spring but which turn green later in the season. The colour change can be delayed by growing this variety in a sunnier position but bright sun will bleach the leaves as shown below. It has pale lavender flowers in mid-summer.

Hosta 'Ginko Craig'.

Hosta 'Gold Haze'.

Hosta 'Gold Standard'.

Hosta *'Gold Standard'* (Banyai, USA, 1976)

This is a sport of *Hosta fortunei* variety *hyacinthina*. In its day it was another ground-breaking introduction and the variety remains extremely popular as a vigorous bright garden plant. It is prone to sporting and many significant varieties are derived from it. It has large gold leaves, colouring best in bright light, with dark green margins. There are pale lavender flowers in mid- to late-summer.

Hosta 'Golden Scepter' (Savory, USA, 1983)

This is a sport of *Hosta* 'Golden Tiara', and another of the popular 'Tiara' series. It is a small variety with a neat mound of almost round, bright gold leaves. It has purple flowers in mid-summer.

Hosta 'Golden Scepter'.

Hosta 'Golden Tiara' (Savory, USA, 1977)

This is a sport of a seedling of *Hosta nakaiana;* it is another very important introduction, leading to the increased popularity of smaller Hostas which is still evident today. It is a small variety of almost round, light-green leaves with yellow margins and purple flowers in mid-summer. The 'Tiara' family offers a good range of colours in smaller varieties and with 'Golden Sceptre' (the gold-leaved form); and 'Golden Tiara'; include also 'Diamond Tiara' (with green leaves edged with white); 'Emerald Tiara' (with golden leaves edged green); 'Grand Tiara' (described next); and 'Platinum Tiara' (with light gold margins edged cream). All are early season varieties, producing low compact mounds, which are all popular garden plants. New varieties continue to be introduced in the 'Tiara' series.

Hosta 'Grand Tiara' (Pollock, USA, 1991)

Tetraploid mutation sported from *Hosta* 'Golden Tiara'. This is a small variety, which has dark green leaves with broad chartreuse to gold margins, and purple flowers in mid-summer.

Hosta 'Great Expectations' (J. Bond, UK, 1988)

Sport of *Hosta sieboldiana* variety *elegans* found in the Savill Gardens in Berkshire, England; it is a very significant introduction with similar varieties available such as *Hostas* 'Borwick Beauty', 'Color Glory' and 'George Smith'. All are large varieties with the *sieboldiana* broad, puckered, blue-green leaves, but with bold, creamy yellow leaf centres. White flowers from early summer. These varieties grow best in less sun than other *sieboldiana* sports. *Hosta* 'Great Expectations' is not the easiest variety to grow but a mature specimen is really spectacular.

Hosta 'Green with Envy' (Chrystal, UK, 2000)

Sport of *Hosta* 'Dawn' (parentage unknown); it is a small variety with round, greenish-yellow leaves and irregular dark green margins and purple flowers in early- to mid-summer.

Hosta 'Golden Tiara'.

Hosta 'Great Expectations'.

Hosta 'Green with Envy'.

Hosta 'Guacamole' (Solberg, USA, 1994)

Sport of *Hosta* 'Fragrant Bouquet' which, like its parent, is an extremely popular large variety because of its attractive foliage and fragrant flowers. The leaves are broad, slightly wavy chartreuse yellow becoming brighter in direct sun, and with wide, quite dark green leaf margins. It has large, pale lavender fragrant flowers in early autumn.

Hosta 'Gypsy Rose' (Anderson, USA)

Tissue culture sport of *Hosta* 'Striptease' introduced in 2000 and registered by the American Hosta Society in 2003. It is a medium variety with dark green, oval leaves with a bright, wide yellow leaf centre, usually separated by a narrow white line, which is not always very obvious. With its lavender flowers in late summer, it is a very distinct, striking and vigorous variety.

Hosta 'Guacamole'.

Hosta 'Gypsy Rose'.

Hosta 'Hadspen Samphire' (Smith, UK)

Hybrid of *Hostas sieboldiana* and 'Kabitan', it was introduced by Eric Smith in the 1970s and registered by the American Hosta Society in 1997. This is a great favourite on our nursery as it is an impressively bright gold colour early in the season. It is a medium variety with long wavy golden leaves which, particularly in a shaded position, will quickly fade to green, though still an attractive compact plant. This Hosta can tolerate a very sunny position when the plant becomes much more compact and the foliage a very bright gold. Deep lavender flowers in late summer.

Hosta 'Halcyon' (Smith, UK)

First generation hybrid of *Hostas tardiflora* and *sieboldiana*; it was raised by Eric Smith in 1961 and registered by the British Hosta and Hemerocallis Society in 1988. This is one of the most outstanding Hostas ever introduced, both in its own right but also for the varieties that have been developed from it. 'Halcyon' is a vigorous medium variety that grows into a dense uniform mound. Its leaves are thick, heart-shaped and a superb silvery blue colour. Despite this colour it can tolerate a sunny position, and it also demonstrates a magnificent golden autumn colour. It has lavender flowers in late summer.

Hosta 'Hadspen Samphire'.

Hosta 'Heat Wave' (van den Top, Holland)

Sport of *Hosta* 'Bright Lights' (from *tokudama*), this medium variety with very thick blue leaves has a broad central splash of gold, forming a neat uniform mound. It is a vigorous variety and a popular choice, but not yet widely available.

Hosta 'Heat Wave'.

Hosta 'Hi-ho Silver' (Walters Gardens, USA, 1977)

Sport of *Hosta* 'Ginko Craig'; this is a small variety with narrow very wavy green leaves and broad pure white margins. It has purple flowers in late summer and is a very popular small variety.

Hosta 'Hi-ho Silver'.

Hosta 'Hydon Sunset'.

Hosta 'High Society' (Hansen, USA, 2004)

Sport of *Hosta* 'June', this very striking medium variety has thick, heart-shaped blue leaves with broad yellow centres, later turning white. Lavender flowers in late summer. When seen for sale, it is hard to resist.

Hosta 'Hydon Sunset' (BHHS, UK)

This is a hybrid of *Hostas gracillima* and 'Wogon Gold'. There is some controversy over the identity of this variety as several similar ones exist. 'Hydon Sunset' was registered by the British Hosta and Hemerocallis Society in 1988 as a small compact plant with gold leaves turning chartreuse as the season progresses. It has purple flowers in mid-summer and is a useful, vigorous small plant for ground cover, border edges, troughs and other containers. In time it can make a wide low clump.

Hosta 'Inniswood' (Inniswood Metro Gardens, USA, 1993)

A sport of *Hosta* 'Sun Glow', originally from *Hosta tokudama*. This is a large variety with heart-shaped, heavily puckered yellow leaves with green margins. It has lavender flowers in early summer.

Hosta 'Inniswood'.

Hosta 'Island Charm'.

Hosta 'Island Charm' (Rasmussen, USA, 1997)

This is a seedling of *Hosta* 'Flambuoyant' (a streaked variety of unknown origin). This small variety makes a neat mound of dark green edged leaves with broad, pale yellow, later white, centres. It is a very eye-catching small variety.

Hosta 'June' (Neo Plants, UK, 1991)

This is one of the most outstanding Hosta varieties and has been a most popular and sought after plant in the United Kingdom since its introduction to the market. It is similarly popular in other countries, and quite rightly, because it is a medium variety and has leaves of heavy substance and subtle colours giving a neat uniform and compact mound that can grow well in wide-ranging conditions. However, with such popularity there has to be controversy and it is suggested that the leaves differ and that there are different forms of 'June'. Certainly the colour and leaf shape vary enormously with age and with situation, and these differences have been described in detail earlier in this book. Our nursery has clumps of the original 'June' growing in demonstration borders and, taking into consideration age and situation and compared with currently available plants, no significant changes have occurred in this variety in over fifteen years. Popular opinion in the United Kingdom favours 'June' grown in the shade; this is the typical 'Halcyon' blue, with broad, apple-green centres with irregular streaks from the margins of the leaves to their centres.

Hosta 'Krossa Regal' (from Japan)

An offspring from *Hosta nigrescens,* it was imported from Japan in the mid-1960s but not registered until 1980. An elegant, very large, vase-shaped variety with large oval slightly wavy, thick, smooth grey green leaves. It grows pale purple-blue, sterile flowers on long stems in late summer. This is a variety which will always be popular, assisted by the knowledge that it is among those varieties whose foliage is the least accessible to slugs and snails

Hosta 'Love Pat' (Aden, USA, 1978)

This is a hybrid of *Hostas* 'Blue Velvet' and 'Blue Vision'. The former is from *Hosta tokudama* but the parentage of the latter is not published. Large variety with thick rounded and cupped, heavily puckered, dark blue green leaves. It has near-white flowers in mid-summer. A popular variety, particularly for its name!

Hosta 'Magic Fire' (van den Top, Holland, 2004)

This sport of *Hosta* 'Sagae' is a large variety with distinctive, flame-patterned, green leaf centres with wide, bright yellow margins. It has pale lavender flowers in late summer.

Hosta 'June'.

Hosta 'Magic Fire'.

Hosta 'Masquerade' (from Japan)

This is a seedling of *venusta,* named by Diana Grenfell in the early 1990s. It is a very small variety with tiny green margined white leaves. It is very prone to produce larger green leaves which need to be frequently removed. It has purple flowers in mid-summer and is ideal for planting in troughs.

Hosta 'Minuteman' (Machen, USA, 1994)

A sport of *Hosta* 'Francee', this is a large variety with crisp, green, slightly shiny, wavy and puckered leaves with broad, pure white margins. It has lavender flowers in late summer and slightly darker and heavier leaves than the very similar *Hosta* 'Patriot'. Both are extremely good and popular varieties though 'Patriot' is the more usually found variety.

Hosta 'Masquerade'.

Hosta 'Minuteman'.

Hosta 'Aureamarginata' (Montana) (Maekawa, Japan)

This sport of *Hosta montana* was found in Japan and named in 1940 by the Japanese botanist Maekawa. It is a very large, spectacular variety and has broad, glossy green leaves with gold margins. There are very pale lavender to white flowers in early summer. It grows best in little sun, and because it emerges so early in the season, needs to be sheltered from cold winds. If such a suitable position is available, this variety is well worth growing.

Hosta 'Moon River' (Lachman, USA, 1991)

A hybrid of *Hostas* 'Crepe Suzette' and 'Blue Moon'; this is a medium variety growing into an attractive low compact mound. It has broad, round, dark green leaves with margins of creamy yellow changing to white. It is particularly useful for low ground cover. There are pale lavender flowers in late summer.

Hosta 'Moon River'.

Hosta 'Moonlight' (Banyai, USA, 1977)

This is a sport of *Hosta* 'Gold Standard'. It is a large variety with yellow, heart-shaped leaves with white margins and is vigorous, quickly making a compact mound. The leaf colour combination is not always popular but the variety is impressive when mature. Pale lavender flowers in late summer.

Hosta 'Mrs Minky' (Hall, USA, 1993)

This is a hybrid of *Hostas minor* and 'Piedmont Gold'. It is a medium variety with chartreuse leaves turning gold in a sunny position and has oval, very wavy-edged leaves twisted at their tips. Pale lavender flowers in mid-summer. The low compact habit of this variety together with its attractive wavy leaves appeals to many gardeners.

Hosta 'Moonlight'.

Hosta 'Mrs Minky'.

Hosta 'Niagara Falls' (Brinka and Petryszyn, USA, 1991)

A hybrid of *Hostas montana microphylla* and 'Sea Drift'. This is a large variety with elongated, dark green, very rippled leaves, which are deeply veined and have a pronounced weeping habit. It has pale lavender flowers in mid-summer and is a great garden plant and superb in a container.

Hosta 'Nicola' (Eason, UK, 1984)

This is a hybrid of similar breeding to the Tardianas and is a medium variety; it is stocked by few nurseries and it cannot be regarded as popular. Nevertheless, it is a useful variety forming a very neat compact mound of smooth, mid-green foliage. Its flowers are particularly attractive and are profuse; they are striped pinky mauve in late summer.

Hosta 'Nicola'.

Hosta 'Night before Christmas' (Machen, USA, 1994)

A tetraploid sport of *Hosta* 'White Christmas', this large variety has neatly tapering, dark green leaves with white centres and pale lavender flowers in late summer. This is a good variety for the garden, and with its slightly weeping habit is particularly attractive in a container. It is relatively early to emerge in the spring and can maintain its good condition until the autumn.

Hosta nigrescens (Japan)

This species is native in Japan and was first named in 1902. It has produced significant offspring, particularly *Hosta* 'Krossa Regal', but has not been so popular itself. It is a very large variety and has an impressive upright habit with thick, slightly puckered blue-green leaves on long erect stems. There are pale lavender flowers in late summer.

Hosta 'On Stage' (Japan)

Very similar or the same as *Hosta Montana* 'Choko Nishiki' which is a natural sport found in the wild in Japan. It is a large variety with slightly wavy, rather thin yellow leaves which have irregular, dark green margins. It has pale lavender flowers in mid-summer.

Hosta 'One Man's Treasure' (Benedict, USA, 1999)

This is a seedling of *Hosta longipes hypoglauca* and is a medium variety with striking red stemmed, very smooth and shiny, dark green leaves. The red of the stem continues into the base of the midrib on the leaf. It forms an attractive dense mound.

Hosta 'On Stage'.

Hosta 'Orange Marmalade' (Solberg, USA, 2002)

This is a tissue culture sport of *Hosta* 'Paul's Glory'. It is an exceptionally good large variety with bright golden, slightly puckered and wavy leaves with very dark green margins. It has pale lavender flowers in late summer and although recently introduced it is already a popular and sought after variety.

Hosta 'Pandora's Box' (Hansen & Shady Oaks, USA, 1996)

A sport of *Hosta* 'Baby Bunting', this is a very small variety with tiny, dark green leaves with wide white centres. It has purple flowers in mid-summer. 'Pandora's Box' can be slow to develop and division at an early stage of growth can lead to unacceptable losses, particularly over the dormant period.

Hosta 'Orange Marmalade'.

Hosta 'Pandora's Box'.

Hosta Paradise Joyce (Fransen, Holland, 1993)

A sport of *Hosta* 'Halcyon', this is a medium variety with thick, smooth, pale gold leaves with blue green margins. It has pale lavender flowers in late summer.

Hosta 'Patriot' (Machen, USA, 1991)

A tetraploid sport of *Hosta* 'Francee', this spectacular and very popular large variety is ideal for brightening up any border. It has very dark green, smooth, slightly wavy leaves with broad, pale creamy yellow margins later turning pure white and also lavender flowers in late summer.

Hosta 'Paul's Glory' (Hofer & Ruh, USA, 1987)

This is a sport of *Hosta* 'Perry's True Blue', which is from *Hosta sieboldiana* . It is an important and popular variety, together with being a parent of some very impressive varieties. Also it is a very large variety with heavy, slightly wavy and corrugated leaves which emerge pale yellowish turning gold to creamy white, depending on exposure to sun, and has dark blue green leaf margins. It has pale lavender flowers in mid-summer.

Hosta 'Paradise Joyce'.

Hosta 'Paul's Glory'.

Hosta 'Peace'.

Hosta 'Peace' (Aden, USA, 1987)

This is a hybrid of *Hosta* 'Blue Hugger' of unknown origin and *Hosta* 'Love Pat'. It is a medium variety with thick, smooth, oval, blue green leaves with yellowish white margins and lavender flowers in late summer.

Hosta 'Pineapple Upsidedown Cake' (Zilis, USA, 1999)

A tissue culture sport of *Hosta* 'Pineapple Poll', this is a large variety with narrow, rippled leaves, first green then bright gold, with narrow, dark green margins. Quick to establish, it makes a bright attractive clump and has lavender flowers in late summer.

Hosta 'Pineapple Upsidedown Cake'.

Hosta plantaginea variety *japonica* (China)

This large variety of *Hosta plantaginea* was originally from China, but is grown widely in Japan. It has glossy and wavy, light green leaves and large, shining, pure white fragrant flowers in late summer to autumn.

Hosta 'Praying Hands' (Williams, USA, 1986)

Parentage not known, which is a shame as this is a most unusual medium variety with a very open upright habit. From the description it does not sound very attractive, but an established specimen plant is very impressive. Leaves are long, narrow and twisted, darkish green with thin, pale yellow margins. It has lavender flowers in late summer.

Hosta 'Radiant Edger' (Zilis, USA, 1990)

This is a tissue culture sport of *Hosta* 'Gold Edger' and is a small variety with heart-shaped, dark green leaves which have broad, pale gold margins. Lavender flowers in mid-summer.

Hosta 'Regal Splendor' (Walters Gardens, USA, 1987)

This is a tissue culture sport of *Hosta* 'Krossa Regal' with a similar, very upright habit. It is a very large variety with grey green leaves and yellow margins turning paler to almost white later; also lavender flowers on tall stems in late summer. These are sterile and so no seed is produced.

Hosta 'Remember Me' (Holland/USA, 2001)

This is a seedling of *Hosta* 'June', raised by van Eijk-Bos and van Ervin and registered by Walters Gardens of USA and is a very popular variety, no doubt assisted by the very attractive name. It is a medium variety with thick, smooth, oval, yellow to creamy white leaves with deep bluish green margins. It has lavender flowers in mid-summer. A stunning plant, but having so little green in the leaves, it is a slow grower.

Hosta 'Radiant Edger'.

Hosta 'Regal Splendor'.

Hosta 'Remember Me'.

Hosta 'Revolution' (van Eijk-Bos, Holland, and Walters Gardens, USA, 2000)

This is a sport of *Hosta* 'Loyalist' and is a medium variety with thick, oval, twisted leaves which are yellow to creamy white centred with green flecks, and broad dark green margins. It has pale lavender flowers in mid-summer. This is an attractive and popular variety which is vigorous and eye-catching. The reverse variegation, with flecked white margins is available as *Hosta* 'Independence', but this is less popular.

Hosta 'Rippled Honey' (Benedict, USA, 1988)

This is a hybrid of *Hosta ventricosa* and *plantaginea* and is a vigorous medium variety with oval, thick, strongly rippled, and very glossy, dark green leaves. It has very pale purple, moderately fragrant, flowers in late summer.

Hosta 'Royal Golden Jubilee' (R. & M. Ford, UK, 2005)

This sport of *Hosta* 'Gold Standard' was introduced by our nursery at the Chelsea Show in the year 2000 in celebration of Her Majesty The Queen's Golden Jubilee. It is a large variety that emerges in the spring with bright golden, wavy leaves with dark green margins. This colour is maintained throughout the season in both sun and shade. In a sunny position the leaves will lighten to a light yellow or creamy white, but too much sun will scorch the leaves. It is available in Europe and the USA as well as in the United Kingdom, and has become a popular variety.

Hosta 'Rippled Honey'.

Hosta 'Royal Golden Jubilee'.

Hosta 'Sarah Kennedy'.

Hosta 'Sagae' (Japan)

This is a natural sport of *Hosta fluctuans* and previously listed as *Hosta fluctuans variegata*. It is a very large spectacular variety which is at its very best early in the season, but it is very difficult to prevent the leaves from scorching later. It has large, thick, wavy, fresh blue-green leaves with broad and irregular very bright gold margins. It has pale lavender flowers in late summer.

Hosta 'Sarah Kennedy' (R. & M. Ford, UK, 2004)

This sport of *Hosta* 'Ginko Craig' was introduced by our nursery in 1997. It is a small but very striking variety with dark green leaves and broad, pure white, wavy margins. It has purple flowers in late summer.

Hosta sieboldiana variety *elegans* (Arends, Germany)

This hybrid of *Hostas fortunei* or *tokudama* and *sieboldiana* has also been known as *robusta*. It was originally described in 1954 and registered by the American Hosta Society in 1987. It is a very large variety with big and thick, very puckered, dark blue green leaves, with white flowers in early summer. It is a very popular, widely available variety, which is the parent of many good modern varieties.

Hosta 'Snowden' (Smith, UK, 1988)

This is a hybrid of the all gold form (*aurea*) of *Hosta fortunei* variety *albopicta* and *Hosta sieboldiana*. It is a very large and upright variety which was registered by the British Hosta and Hemerocallis Society in 1988. It has huge, erect and thick oval, slightly puckered, sage-green to blue green leaves. White flowers in early- to mid-summer. It is a vigorous, popular and widely available variety.

Hosta 'So Sweet' (Aden, USA, 1986)

This is a hybrid from *Hosta* 'Fragrant Bouquet'. It is a medium variety with oval, slightly glossy, smooth but wavy edged, mid-green leaves with quite wide yellow margins, later turning paler. It has large, fragrant off-white flowers in late summer to early autumn.

Hosta 'Split Milk' (Seaver, USA, 1999)

This is a seedling of *Hosta sieboldiana* origin. It was raised in the 1980s and registered by the American Hosta Society in 1999. It is a most unusual, large variety with a very appropriate name as the thick, moderately puckered, pale blue green heart-shaped leaves have streaks and splashes of pure white randomly over the leaves. It has white flowers in early summer.

Hosta 'Stained Glass' (Hansen, USA, 1999)

This is a tissue culture sport of *Hosta* 'Guacamole'. Large variety with quite thick, slightly wavy and puckered gold leaves with dark green margins. It has large, fragrant, very pale lavender flowers in late summer to autumn. It is a very striking and vigorous variety.

Hosta 'Stiletto' (Aden, USA, 1987)

This is a hybrid of *Hosta* 'Amy Aden' and a variegated *Hosta pulchella*. It is a small variety with narrow, lance-shaped, strongly rippled, medium green leaves with creamy gold margins. It has lavender flowers in late summer.

Hosta 'Striptease' (Thompson, USA, 1991)

This is a tetraploid sport of *Hosta* 'Gold Standard' and is a large variety with slightly puckered, heart-shaped, dark green leaves with greenish gold centres, separated by a narrow white margin. It has pale lavender flowers in mid-summer and is a very popular and widely-available variety from which many unusual sports have been raised.

Hosta 'Stained Glass'.

Hosta 'Stiletto'.

Hosta 'Sum and Substance' (Aden, USA, 1980)

This is a triploid of unknown parentage. It is a huge variety with very large and very heavy textured, moderately puckered, glossy green to yellow leaves. These will be the lighter colour in more sunny situations. This is a remarkable variety and is extremely popular for its huge leaves, general robustness and the enormous clump size, which in our own nursery has reached 9½ ft (nearly 3m) in diameter. It is also the parent of many excellent sports and seedlings.

Hosta 'Sum and Substance'.

Hosta 'Summer Music' (Klehm, USA, 1998)

This is the sport of *Hosta* 'Shade Master' and is a medium variety, having leaves with yellow to creamy white centres, and broad pale- to mid-green margins. It has pale lavender flowers in mid-summer and is a vigorous plant but is best in a less sunny position.

Hosta 'Summer Music'.

Hosta 'Tambourine' (Lachman, USA, 1987)

This is a hybrid of a *Hosta* 'Resonance' cross and *Hosta* 'Halcyon'. Registered by the American Hosta Society but introduced well before that date, it is a great favourite of mine and I cannot understand why it is not more popular. It is a large upright variety with lovely glaucous blue green, oval slightly wavy and puckered thick leaves, with yellow to creamy white margins, and very attractive purple flowers in late summer which should make it even more desirable.

Hosta 'Tambourine'.

Hosta 'Thunderbolt' (Crowder, USA, 1998)

This is a sport of *Hosta sieboldiana* variety *elegans*. Large variety with thick, heart-shaped, slightly wavy and puckered, thick, blue-green leaves, with a central splash of yellow to creamy white. It has white flowers in early summer and is similar to *Hosta* 'Dream Weaver'.

Hosta tokudama form *aureo-nebulosa* (Japan)

This natural sport of *Hosta tokudama* was named in 1940 in Japan and registered by the American Hosta Society in 1987. It is a medium variety with thick, rounded and puckered, blue green leaves with irregular beige to gold centres much streaked with blue green from the leaf margins. It has off white flowers in mid-summer.

Hosta 'Thunderbolt'.

Hosta tokudama form *aurea-nebulosa.*

Hosta tokudama form
flavocircinalis.

Hosta tokudama form *flavocircinalis* (Japan)

This is a natural sport of *Hosta tokudama*, named in 1940 in Japan and registered by the American Hosta Society in 1987. It is a medium variety with thick, rounded and puckered, blue-green leaves with broad and irregular beige to gold margins. It is almost a smaller version of *Hosta* 'Frances Williams' and has off white flowers in mid-summer.

Hosta 'Touch of Class' (Hansen, USA, 1999)

This is a tetraploid sport of *Hosta* 'June' and is a medium variety with thick, heart-shaped, blue leaves with medium gold to chartreuse centres. It is a very tough and striking variety, arguably rather similar to, but not quite better than its celebrated parent. It has pale lavender flowers in late summer.

Hosta 'Twilight' (van Eijk-Bos et al, Holland, 1997)

This is a sport of *Hosta fortunei* variety *aureamarginata*. It has shiny, smooth green leaves with a bluish, sometimes almost purplish, tinge and broad yellow to creamy yellow margins. Lavender flowers in mid-summer. This can be a rather hard variety to establish but a good specimen plant can be quite stunning.

Hosta venusta (Korea)

This is a species originating from an island off South Korea, and described by the Japanese botanist Maekawa in 1935. It is a very small variety with smooth, but slightly wavy-edged, dark green leaves, which form a dense spreading mound. It has purple flowers in early summer and is popular for rockeries and troughs, and important as the parent for many sports and seedlings.

Hosta 'Twilight'.

Hosta venusta.

Hosta 'War Paint' (Naylor Creek, USA, 2005)

This is a tissue culture sport of *Hosta* 'Niagara Falls', and is a very choice, large variety with great impact, particularly in the spring. It has large oval, strongly rippled and cascading greenish-white to white centred leaves with margins of two toned green and produces pale lavender flowers in mid-summer.

Hosta 'War Paint'.

Hosta 'Whirlwind' (Kulpa, USA, 1989)

This is a possible sport from *Hosta fortunei* variety *hyacinthina* and is one of the really important Hostas, very vigorous with thick foliage making an excellent popular garden plant. Medium variety with wavy and twisted, moderately puckered, thick dark green leaves with broad irregular centres of creamy yellow, darkening to green later in the season – particularly if planted in a shaded position. Lavender flowers in late summer.

Hosta 'Whirlwind'.

Hosta 'Wide Brim' (Aden, USA, 1979)

This is a hybrid of *Hostas* 'Bold One' and 'Bold Ribbons'. It is a medium variety with oval, puckered and wavy, mid- to dark-green leaves, with wide yellow margins which lighten to cream It has pale lavender flowers in late summer. This has been a very popular plant and used to be one of our nursery's best-selling varieties – probably a casualty of more recent introductions. It is still a good vigorous variety with bright foliage making a neat dense clump.

Hosta 'Wolverine' (Wilkins, USA, 1995)

This is a sport of a *Hosta* 'Dorset Blue' hybrid. It is a medium variety with long, smooth, slightly wavy-edged, blue-green leaves with bold, pale creamy yellow margins, making a dense, slightly weeping mound. Early to emerge in the spring, it is particularly attractive in the early part of the year. It has pale purple flowers in late summer.

Hosta 'Wide Brim'.

Hosta 'Wolverine'.

Further information

FURTHER READING

Grenfell, D. *The Gardener's Guide to Growing Hostas* (B.T. Batsford)

Grenfell, D. & Shadrack, M. *The Colour Encyclopedia of Hostas* (Timber Press)

Schmid, W. George *The Genus Hosta* (B.T. Batsford)

Zilis, Mark R. *The Hostapedia – An Encyclopedia of Hostas* (Q&Z Nursery, Inc.)

USEFUL WEBSITES

The American Hosta Society
www.americanhostasociety.org

The British Hosta and Hemerocallis Society(BHHS)
www.Hostahem.org.uk

The Royal Horticultural Society
www.rhs.org.uk

United States Hosta Library
www.Hostalibrary.org

General index

Index of Hosta species and varieties